THE UNKNOWN CIA

Also by Russell Jack Smith
The Secret War   1986

THE UNKNOWN CIA

My Three Decades with the Agency

RUSSELL JACK SMITH
Foreword by Richard Helms

PERGAMON-BRASSEY'S
International Defense Publishers, Inc.

Washington • New York • London • Oxford
Beijing • Frankfurt • São Paulo • Sydney • Tokyo • Toronto

Copyright © 1989 Pergamon-Brassey's International
Defense Publishers, Inc.

Pergamon-Brassey's books are available at special discounts for bulk purchases for sales promotions, premiums, fund-raising, or educational use through the
Special Sales Director,
Macmillan Publishing Company
866 Third Avenue, New York, N.Y. 10022.

Editorial Offices
Pergamon-Brassey's International Defense Publishers, Inc.
8000 Westpark Drive, Fourth Floor
McLean, Virginia 22102

British Library Cataloguing in Publication Data
Smith, Russell Jack
    The unknown CIA : my three decades with the agency.
    1. United States. Central Intelligence Agency
    I. Title
    327.1'2'0973
    ISBN 0-08-036743-7

Library of Congress Cataloging-in-Publication Data
Smith, Russell Jack.
    The unknown CIA : my three decades with the Agency / Russell Jack Smith : foreword by Richard Helms.
        p. cm.
    ISBN 0-08-036743-7 : $18.95 (est.)
    1. Smith, Russell Jack. 2. Intelligence officers—United States—Biography. 3. United States. Central Intelligence Agency—History. I. Title.
UB271.U52S657   1989
327.1'2'092—dc20
[B]   89-32288
                                                                                            CIP

10 9 8 7 6 5 4 3 2 1
Printed in the United States of America

To the others who served proudly

Contents

Foreword

When the world learned the American government had established that the Libyan regime was secretly building a chemical weapons plant, with the consequent implication that such weapons might be used in worldwide terrorist attacks, many Americans and Europeans accepted that finding as true but few understood how it had been determined. Obviously there had been no proclamation from Tripoli—hot denials instead—and no eyewitness inspections by objective observers. TV news broadcasts had told the world that espionage had come into play and possibly some intercepts and overhead photography. But it is a long span from secret reports and photos to a conclusion firm enough to support an official government statement.

That conclusion had been reached and affirmed by Washington intelligence analysts, by men and women sitting at desks sorting, sifting, and patterning secret evidence into a matrix that carried conviction. This work—analysis—is the *bottomline* of intelligence work. This is where all the arcane techniques of intelligence come together. This is the unknown, the neglected side of the profession that has been caricatured into absurdity by writers of spy thrillers. This is the subject of this fine and overdue book.

The author of *The Unknown CIA: My Three Decades with the Agency* is a longtime colleague, Russell Jack Smith. His qualifications for detailing the beginnings and the maturing of CIA's analytic service are exemplary. He was present at the founding of the Agency in 1947 and worked closely with all the directors of Central Intelligence, including myself, for the ensuing quarter century. He directed the work of CIA analysts during the Cuban Missile Crisis, the Arab-Israeli Six-Day War, and the innumerable highs and lows of the Vietnam War. He relates the role of CIA in each of these historic events with rich and vivid detail.

Perhaps the greatest service this book performs is to portray the workaday operations and internal atmosphere of the Agency. It describes with the pride of an intelligence professional the unwavering objectivity and dedication to accuracy of the mostly unknown intelligence analysts. This is indeed "the unknown CIA."

Richard Helms
Director of Central Intelligence
1966–1973

Proud Service

1

I spent some thirty years in the Intelligence Service. For me and, I believe, for most of those who served with me in the Central Intelligence Agency, these were years of high meaning—serious work in the American interest.

I was and remain proud of my work there . . . I believe in the importance to the nation of the function that the Agency served. I still do, without regrets, without qualms, without apology.

—RICHARD HELMS before the Rockefeller Commission, January 16, 1975

It happened again at my wife's high school reunion. Amid the joys and pangs of delayed recognition, a woman, lovely and fresh in her 60s, asked me lightly, "And what do you do?" Replying with a lightness matching hers, I said, "I served in the CIA for twenty-seven years. I was a deputy director." Then the look came in her eyes, the look that always comes. How to describe it? Too complex to be encompassed by a single word, its main ingredients seem to be a dollop of surprise, a dash of suspicion, and an overflowing measure of curiosity and piqued interest. I had seen it so many times I could almost follow the tumbling processes of her mind as she recalled those newspaper accounts—CIA involvement in assassinations, CIA drug experiments, dozens of CIA-engineered coups in foreign countries hither and yon. Next, experience told me, would come a follow-up question. Gazing appreciatively at the sunny blue eyes of this gentle creature, I felt

1

certain the question would be a soft one. And it was. "Did you enjoy that?" "Very much," I replied. "I had a wonderful career."

Now the eyes acquired the next look: unquenched curiosity checked by courtesy and uncertainty as to her right to ask certain questions. I knew that she had not asked what she really wanted to know; if unrestrained, she would have posed the question: "What was it *really* like inside CIA?" I could do little in the middle of a cocktail reception to meet her unvoiced query squarely, but I ventured a little way toward meeting it by recounting a family incident.

"You know, my youngest son, when he was about ten, came home late Sunday afternoon, and said, 'Dad, it seems to me all the fathers in the neighborhood complain every Sunday about having to go back to work on Monday. But I never hear you complain about it. Why is that?' And I said to him, 'Because I can hardly wait to get back there and take up where I left off.' "

My lovely acquaintance smiled, and I hoped this reflected both enjoyment of the perceptivity in that ten-year-old's question and an appreciation of the zest and keen involvement I felt while serving in CIA. Either she was partially satisfied or my story touched a motherly chord because her next question was, "How many children do you have?"

In every respect this resembled a hundred such encounters I have had since retiring from CIA. A slightly different conversation occurred with an old academic friend, then the dean of humanities at a prestigious university of technology. "Tell me, what do you say when people ask about your profession?" I answered simply, "I tell them I am a retired senior CIA officer." He paused and asked almost gingerly, "And what kind of response do you get?" The expectations underlying his questions were clear: he expected people to react sneeringly or angrily. I was pretty certain that many of his colleagues, members of the academic community who had become deeply alienated in the sixties by the Vietnam War and the Johnson and Nixon administrations' equivocal handling of it, would so respond. But I had not, for one reason or another encountered that. "People usually are polite but curious," I said. "They seem to sense the hysteria of the press, and they want to know how much to believe." He nodded understandingly. He, too, would like to know how much to believe.

Most Americans observe the operations of their national government in two ways, neither likely to give them a charitable understanding of its purposes. The first perspective comes from the American newspapers and TV that provide new evidence every day of the venality, confusion, and general wrongheadedness that seem to abound in Washington. The other perspective, often obtained firsthand but equally likely to evoke distaste, comes through visits to the local post office or from exchanges with the Internal Revenue Service. These perspectives, when combined with the traditional frontier mythology that still permeates American minds and supports an antigovernment ethos, makes it exceedingly difficult to understand why any intelligent person would elect to spend a lifetime working in Washington, let alone enjoy it and find it deeply satisfying.

But I did.

Well, yes, you say, maybe in CIA being a spy. As all of us have observed, the words *spy*, *espionage*, and *clandestine* precipitate a chemical reaction that causes eyes to light up, hearts to quicken, and ears to point forward. The Byzantine, surrealistic confections of John Le Carre and a host of lesser entertainers have exploited a normal human interest in secret shenanigans and have fastened a grossly distorted, frivolous image upon a serious, highly professional activity. Being a "CIA spy" surely must have brought me such standard accessories as a Lambretta pistol, an Aston Martin or Ferrari (take your choice), and a clutch of panting, lascivious females who harbored a deep reluctance to keep themselves fully clothed. Not to mention a knack for laconic, cryptic speech.

I suppose I ought to feel the same mingling of sorrow one experiences when telling a wondering six-year-old child, hoping against hope, that indeed there is no Santa Claus, but duty obliges me to rise above it. I will put it bluntly. CIA is not like that. Nor, I might add, is the KGB.

To begin, the main task of CIA when it was established in 1947 was not espionage or covert action. These are ancillary activities added later to the CIA charter. The essential task of CIA remains to this day to *centralize*—assemble in one place in Washington, D.C.—all the foreign intelligence gathered by the many arms of the U.S. government with missions and facilities overseas. This is what the *Central* of the Central Intelligence Agency refers to. The derring-do and cloaks and daggers were tacked on later when the Cold War began to intensify. It surely is one of life's ironies that CIA's secret clandestine activities have been its most highly publicized—blazoned may be a better word—while its reporting and analytic chores have been virtually kept a secret from the American public.

The Central Intelligence Agency was established in the late 1940s when the disastrous "surprise" attack on Pearl Harbor was still fresh in the minds of American leaders. Investigators have demonstrated abundantly that enough information was at hand in the summer and autumn of 1941 to make sound predictions about Japanese intentions. But the information lay about in bits and pieces, some in Hawaii where the Army and Navy commanders were studiously keeping it secret from each other, and some scattered around Washington, distributed unevenly among the State Department and the Army and Navy. No one group had all the pieces of the jigsaw puzzle in one place. It seemed clear to later investigators in the forties and fifties—and it has seemed clear to CIA analysts ever since—that if all the separate pieces, odd-shaped and different-sized though they were, had been placed on one table in Washington, a skilled, trained person could have put the puzzle together. President Roosevelt could have been properly warned, and American forces at Pearl Harbor and elsewhere in the Pacific could have taken protective action. This is what CIA was organized

4

to do in 1947 and what it has done with considerable success ever since.

What historical process caused CIA to be identified primarily with covert activity while the overt remained obscure? More than any other single factor, it was the hard lessons of the Cold War learned by American policy makers shortly after World War II came to a close in 1945. Confronted with the steady and growing pressures of Soviet-backed political and paramilitary forces in France, Italy, Greece, and Hungary, Washington looked about for the means to respond. Against these "local" forces, clothing themselves with democratic aims and slogans of varying shades of validity, direct action by U.S. military force was neither feasible nor desirable. The alternative: supply the legitimate government with money, material, and if necessary, guidance to survive these Soviet-supported threats. But do it covertly. Why covertly? Because directly linking the United States with these internal struggles would make the local governments appear to be U.S. puppets, and add credibility to the pretensions of the dissidents that they were democratic, justice-seeking groups unsupported by any foreign governments. The next question was: who in Washington should take on this job? Neither the Department of State nor the Pentagon had any interest, let alone capability, but there was the fledgling Central Intelligence Group, and there was a remnant of an Office of Strategic Services (OSS) espionage unit. The solution was at hand and the task assigned.

From the outset the job was a huge one, requiring large infusions of funds and substantial numbers of people to plan and run the operations. During the following decade the mission expanded to global proportions. The successes of CIA covert action in Iran and Guatemala, as well as several less-heralded ones, seemed to convince U.S. policy makers that here was the ideal Cold War weapon, less arduous than standard diplomacy and more effective. At this moment the figure of Allen Dulles emerged from the traditional anonymity of espionage and became identified as the

"American spymaster." Tweedy, patrician, pipe-smoking, he exuded an aura of well-bred mystery and reassuring solidity. His personage bestowed legitimacy and propriety upon the Agency. But unfortunately his image also stamped CIA indelibly as simply a nest of spies.

It is intriguing to speculate how the fortunes of CIA might have differed if clandestine operators like Allen Dulles, Richard Helms, and William Colby had not led the Agency at any time. Certainly not all the differences would have been beneficial, but some might have been. If a prestigious academician of the quality, say, of Vannevar Bush or James Conant had taken over the leadership of CIA in 1947, the clandestine services could have remained in relative obscurity while the research and analysis side could have taken on some of the qualities of its director, and CIA would have been seen as a source of thoughtful, dispassionate judgments on world affairs. This would have placed the emphasis within CIA where it was intended, and obscurity would have served the purposes of the clandestine services very well. Tight security would have been easier to maintain and the success of sensitive operations enhanced. Despite the American experience of the past decade, it is not inevitable that U.S. covert action programs be emblazoned in daily newspaper headlines. Other democracies with civil liberty claims as lofty as ours have managed to strike a balance between freedom of the press and essential security in national security affairs.

The British provide probably the best example of an open democracy that can, for the most part, keep secret affairs secret. The fundamental difference between British and American practices regarding their national espionage organizations was once the topic for discussion between Allen Dulles and President John F. Kennedy. Shortly after completion of the CIA headquarters building in Langley, Virginia, a large green highway sign was erected on Dolley Madison Boulevard to mark the entrance. At the same time, Robert Kennedy, the newly elected president's brother, took a house a scant third of a mile away, and the route he took daily to work into Washington caused him to pass directly under this sign, reading "Central Intelligence Agency." His astonishment was matched by his disapproval. The nation's spy headquarters advertising itself!

When he reached his office, Robert shared his shock with the president, who immediately picked up his telephone and said to Allen Dulles, "Allen, that sign you have out there, I want it taken down. You know, the British don't advertise their secret service like that." Mr. Dulles was as aware of this as the president. At that time the chief of the secret service was never named in the British press, and his organization huddled in Whitehall among other obscure government offices. But Dulles felt his situation was different, and he protested, pointing out that CIA's location was charted on every Esso and National Geographic map of Washington. Moreover, he explained, the sign helped delivery men bringing supplies to the Agency. The president was not moved by this reasoning, so like any other bureaucrat, Allen Dulles acceded to his superior officer's instruction. But also like other bureaucrats when the directive is uncongenial, he did not act immediately. Meanwhile, Robert Kennedy passed under the sign twice a day on his way to and from work, and after several days the president called again. This time his tone was peremptory. "Allen, if that sign is not taken down right away, I'm coming out Saturday morning to take it down myself!" Dulles capitulated, and the sign came down at midnight on Friday. As a consequence, for the next dozen years no sign stood at the CIA entrance except for a small one reading, "Bureau of Public Roads," CIA's next-door neighbor. This seeming absurdity afforded the *Washington Post* wondrous amusement annually.

John and Robert Kennedy were not the only ones who felt it was a mistake to advertise CIA's presence. Within the Agency, many clandestine service officers disliked the well-publicized new building, with its two easily surveilled entrances. They would have preferred to keep their offices in the shabby World War II temporary buildings down by the Lincoln Memorial. Indeed, some clandestine service officers would have liked very much to sever organizational ties with the rest of the Agency—cut the direct link with the analytic, technical, and administrative sides—and become less visible.

It was out of this family of ideas, no doubt, that Richard Helms would on occasion tell outsiders that the clandestine service really occupied a supporting, not primary, role in CIA. Like his predecessors Allen Dulles and John McCone, Helms often gave get-acquainted lunches in his private dining room for American corporation executives, ambassadors, senators, and other influential people. This enabled these dignitaries to meet the CIA top command, exchange views about world affairs, and come to understand the Agency better. They also got an excellent lunch. Seated before a handsome lamb chop, Dick presented each of his deputies and one or two other senior officers around the table to the distinguished guest. When he came to me, he frequently said, "Jack is the deputy director for intelligence. He does what the Agency was really set up to do. He is responsible for piecing together all the bits of information we get and making meaningful reports and analyses out of them."

At this point I usually wore a modest smile. My fellow deputy directors—Tom Karamessines, the deputy director for plans (read "espionage and covert operations") and Carl Duckett, the deputy director for science and technology (read "scientific research and development of such technical devices as the U-2 and satellite cameras")—usually produced smiles more knowing than modest. Both administered budgets several times the size of mine, and both basked in the knowledge that their activities were synonymous with CIA in most people's minds. They were content to have Dick Helms describe the Agency as primarily an analysis and reporting organization so long as that image did not alter their acknowledged roles as the muscle and fiber of CIA.

Public and official acceptance of this image of CIA as simply a spy factory did not sit well with the analysts and estimators who believed themselves to be carrying out the Agency's essential task while the "spooks" not only got the glory but sometimes landed themselves in messes that drew harsh criticism and—through association—lessened the credibility of CIA reporting and analysis. The press has steadily pictured the Agency as a monolithic organization in which all employees are "CIA agents"—even including such people as Frank Terpil, who in his Agency career was a "Commo tech," a repairman for communications equipment like telex machines. The reality, however, is that CIA is essentially a conglomerate, a clutch of organizations performing allied tasks. In the first ten to fifteen years the division between the separate offices was almost water-tight and sometimes hostile. Clandestine service officers often regarded the analysts as walking sieves, leaking hard-won espionage reports from every pore. The analysts responded by characterizing the "spooks" as reckless blunderers who were paranoid about secrecy, especially as it pertained to their reports, which, in the view of the analysts, were often trivial and second- or third-rate compared to State Department reporting or the intercepted communications of the National Security Agency. Over the years a degree of understanding and mutual respect was established, but it was really not until the directorship of Richard Helms that CIA became well integrated, with all elements working synchronously and interdependently. It was an achievement in which I feel I played a helping part.

If the status of the Directorate of Intelligence (the DDI as it was known within the Agency) had some resemblance to that of a stepchild, or perhaps more precisely a lightly regarded maiden aunt, this came about through a historical development running crosswise to the original concept. It probably owed something also to the DDI itself in failing to exploit opportunity. Probably no national intelligence organization has ever done better the task the DDI set out to do, but at the same time the DDI was not as effective as it could have been because its leaders, including myself, did not clearly perceive its optimum role in relation to the rest of the Agency. In its analysis and reporting the DDI tried in a way to rise above CIA, to shed its clandestine intelligence cloak and to

9

take on a disembodied voice of purest detachment and objectivity. In doing so, it often became so rarified, so academic in tone that it lost its legitimate claim to attention in Washington as the voice of CIA, a unique intelligence organization with information and analytic skills not to be found elsewhere.

But this observation is really a counsel of perfection. Despite its imperfections, its distortions of mission, its excesses and lapses, and its failure to represent itself forthrightly and accurately to the American people, the Central Intelligence Agency during its first twenty-five years became unquestionably the finest national intelligence organization in the world. It may still be, for that matter, but I am no longer in a position to say so with assurance. I can speak, however, with earned confidence about the first quarter-century.

When it came time for me to retire and reenter the outside world, leaving behind the shared conviction of my colleagues that CIA was in the main a fine organization staffed by people who combined high ability with intense dedication to the tasks of the Agency and to the nation which it served, I was appalled by the contrasting image the media were presenting daily. Each morning, as I sat at my breakfast table, seeking to subdue the old fire-horse instinct to rush off to the office as I had done for twenty-seven years, I read the *Washington Post* with its daily potpourri of half-truths, distortions, and sensational accounts of all the derelictions CIA was said to have committed throughout its entire history. Most of these alleged misdeeds I had no knowledge about; nearly all of them, when compared to the great tasks that constitute CIA's main mission, seemed minor in importance. And as I read the painful accounts of Director William Colby's beleaguered testimony before one congressional investigative committee after another, I found myself muttering aloud, "Bill, for God's sake why don't you make just two points: (1) all the allegations lumped together, even if admitted to be entirely true, would constitute no more than 1 percent of the Agency's total and highly laudable performance; and (2) each of the activities cited as willful or illegal operations were in fact ordered or sanctioned by the National Security Council." The press did not report Colby as having made these points.

I had had a conversation with Daniel Patrick Moynihan while sitting in the ambassador's office in New Delhi one morning that convinced me that both CIA and the nation would be better served if the Agency's purposes and accomplishments were more widely known and better understood by Americans. Our conversation began as it had many times before in the splendor of the ambassadorial office, the only comfortable place in the showy but inefficient New Delhi Embassy designed by Edward Durrell Stone. Indira Gandhi was again telling her people that the latest civil disturbance in some remote part of India had been created by CIA agents, agents who were to be found, according to Madame Gandhi, beneath every *charpoy* and behind every *neem* tree. (Indeed, so frequent and so obvious had these charges become that the *Times of India* ran a front-page cartoon depicting a minion reporting to the prime minister, "Last week the CIA was responsible for a demonstration in Allahabad, a riot in Calcutta, and a typhoon in Orissa.") When I had finished reassuring the ambassador that these latest allegations were, as usual, preposterous, I launched into the larger theme of CIA's basic mission, *centralizing* intelligence analysis. Knowing Moynihan's professional interest in economic and sociological research, I mentioned some of the sophisticated methodologies we had developed in the Office of Economic Research for analysis in those fields as they applied to foreign countries. Pat Moynihan was fascinated—and astonished. "I didn't know you fellows did work like that. You ought to tell people about that sort of thing."

When I left, I reflected that Moynihan's astonishment was itself astonishing. Here was this Harvard scholar and oft-time presidential appointee who had never discovered that CIA was not merely a spy organization and who thought our only game was skulduggery. Despite his years of service as a White House staff officer and subcabinet official, he had remained unaware of the one thing that makes CIA unique among the world's intelligence agencies: its ability to perform highly sophisticated research and to produce independent estimative judgments.

I further reflected that the fault was not really Pat Moynihan's; it was at least in part CIA's. If there had been a small set of books standing on university library shelves that described the effective role CIA has performed in support of national security policy over the years, men like Moynihan could have informed themselves about this side of the Agency before coming to Washington. But no such shelf of books existed. Without prohibiting the writing and publishing of such books, the Agency has for security reasons created an atmosphere that inhibits their publication. There are a few exceptions. Sherman Kent's book, *Strategic Intelligence for American World Policy*, was published in 1946 during his Yale interlude between OSS and CIA, and although it makes a valuable contribution, it does so largely as a blueprint for what he hoped national strategic intelligence might become rather than what it became. Harry Howe Ransom's books are, by design, the views of a scholar *outside* CIA. Ray Cline has written a useful book, *Secrets, Spies, and Scholars*, which belongs on the small shelf I have in mind, and Ray's career and mine were nearly contemporaneous. But more than one perspective would be useful, it seemed to me, when trying to describe this organization so veiled by mystery and misunderstanding. I decided that when I retired from active service I would undertake to write an account of my own career in CIA that might take its place on that small shelf of books my mind envisaged.

On the day I was to complete the formalities of my retirement from CIA, including a farewell call on Director William Colby, my breakfast companion as usual was the *Washington Post*. An unsavory accompaniment to breakfast it was. This was early summer 1974, and the outpouring of Watergate effluent was in full flood. The *Washington Post* was proudly displaying and flexing its newfound muscles for investigative journalism by twisting, stretching, and bending each new bit of flotsam to expose otherwise unseen nuances. CIA's suspected involvement seemed to give the *Post*

12

special zest for these investigative revelations. As the year had worn on, each day produced some new disclosure, often an incident from the 1950s that fueled more dark speculations about CIA machinations. I was appalled by the irresponsible reporting, the twisting of evidence, the blatant use of unfounded assumption, and the lack of perspective, historical or otherwise. I knew for a fact that CIA analysts who turned in such sloppy, loosey-goosey work would have been fired. More than ever the record needed to be set straight. At least, straighter.

Despite the pounding William Colby was absorbing daily from the press and congressional committees, I found him on my final visit to be the same as I had known him for a dozen years or more, impersonally affable and bloodlessly cool about his situation and the Agency's. "The only thing to do," he said in his laconic way, "is to lay out all the facts, disclose all the mistakes, not hold any back, and in a while, it will all blow over." This seemed to me a woefully naive estimate of the gluttonous appetite of the American press and public for spy trivia, but I had come to say goodbye, not to argue.

I broached my ideas about a book based on my career in CIA. Colby said something kindly about its being "a good one." I reminded him that I would need his sanction to obtain ready access to CIA headquarters and to files for background material. (One must understand that despite my recently surrendered status as a senior CIA officer with twenty-seven years' honorable service I now had no more privilege in entering the Langley building than a passerby off the street; I was obliged to sign the same form as any other visitor declaring my U.S. citizenship, and I needed an escort while walking down the corridors or indeed while visiting the men's room.)

In response to my reminder, Bill Colby shook his head. "Can't do that. If we give you support everyone will think the book is biased in our favor."

This startled me. "My God, Bill, nobody is going to accuse me of absolute impartiality after twenty-seven years in this place.

13

The book will have to establish its own credibility by the way I treat facts and events."

But Colby was not to be budged. His mind was set. So I took my leave and walked out the front door of CIA headquarters into retirement.

Roughly speaking, there are two ways, I suppose, of recording a professional career. One is to gather the facts gleaned from memorandums, files, diaries, letters, and published materials, and then write a documented account complete with names, dates, and recorded events. The other is to rely on memories and impressions surrounding major happenings, the kind that burn deep, indelible impressions, and then write a memoir that moves from highlight to highlight, the peaks and valleys of a career, recapturing the vivid moments and emotions. The first, of course, has the greater value for historians, but the second has the redeeming hope of greater appeal for the general reader who wants mostly to know *what it was like.*

I decided to write the second kind, based more on memory than documents, and then set about restructuring my daily life and work habits to make this feasible. My family and I had just returned to Washington after three years abroad so I had some sizeable social and cultural adjustments to make as well as adjustments that accompany the decompression of retirement. Meanwhile, as 1974 wore on, post-Watergate hysteria mounted and widened. Allegations of CIA wrongdoing tumbled over one another in their profusion, and soon the American press (the most immediate exemplar for me being the *Washington Post*) began to treat as established fact that CIA had over twenty-five years set itself up as an independent body, answerable in no way to Congress, the White House, or American traditions of truth and fair play, and had undertaken through malice or whim, or both, to assassinate national leaders far and wide, to topple the governments of small countries at random, to tap telephones and open the mail of U.S. citizens, and for the hell of it, to administer drugs to unsuspecting persons and observe the result. At times, the press seemed to have

14

difficulty in deciding whether to present CIA as a comic figure, a mass of bumbling ineptitudes or as a terrifyingly effective force (it is difficult to be both). But it never wavered on the central theme: CIA was out of control.

This was so contrary to what I knew to be true as to leave me gasping. All CIA's power and authority derive directly from the president, and anyone who entertains seriously the notion that CIA could assassinate a leader or topple a foreign government contrary to White House order or permission simply does not understand how power is disposed in Washington. As for Congress, I had personally spent hundreds of hours and dozens of full days briefing congressional committees, and I knew how precious the CIA top command felt good congressional relations were, if only to prevent the kind of surprise and dismay that causes problems when congressmen turn their attention to the CIA budget. But in the firestorm that Watergate started, no voices of common sense or reason could be heard above the roar. And as it went on and on and on, with congressional investigations and politically tinged and leaked reports, I began to feel that it was useless to write the book I had in mind until a calmer day dawned. It would be futile to try to answer the half-truths, distortions, and lies one by one while trying to separate from them the legitimate charges. In any event, I was not in a position to undertake such a task.

Meanwhile, personal circumstances and the persistent intrusion of personal and professional interests slowed my progress even as my dismay deepened as calumny and disgrace showered daily on CIA. Dark thoughts came to mind, including the painful question: have I wasted my professional life by serving with an institution now held at best to be worthless and at worst to be deeply damaging to the American tradition and spirit? Then I remembered the insightful question my ten-year-old son had asked me about returning to work on Monday morning. And I remembered another occasion, a glorious Saturday morning in May when the willow-green grass of our meadow prinked and preened in the brisk sunshine and the dogwood trees at the edge of the woods sported

15

white-petaled mantles. It was a morning that demanded some kind of family excursion, a picnic or at least a baseball game in the meadow. But the direct-line CIA telephone by my bed had summoned me to deal with some crisis or another. Disappointment among the boys gave way quickly to commiseration over this unkind development. "That's all right," I said. "You fellows go have a good time while I stand watch on the ramparts." It was a poor joke, even a vainglorious one, but it held a kernel of sincerity. I *did* feel I was performing a useful and important service. I *did* feel part of a band of people who were devoting themselves to help guard the country's security and the security of their families and friends.

And I was by no means unique among CIA career officers, not even unusual. I don't suppose many of them would voice their attitude toward the Agency and its mission in quite the way I have, but almost all the men and women I worked with gave evidence at one time or another of their deep dedication to patriotic service. They believed in CIA's purpose and its mission; they believed in its value to the country. The organization, at least when I left it, was filled with talented, spirited people who enjoyed their daily work and found it deeply fulfilling. Deep in their bones they knew they belonged to a highly professional institution engaged in an essential service for the U.S. government and American people. A proud service. This is the subject and theme of this book.

Early Years

2

I got into intelligence strictly by chance. By choice, I remained for more than twenty-five years.

When World War II reached in and touched the lives of all Americans I was doing exactly what I wanted to do and what I intended to do for the rest of my life. Moreover, I was doing it in ideal surroundings. I was teaching English literature at Williams College in Williamstown, Massachusetts. All through college at Miami University in Oxford, Ohio, and four years of graduate school at Cornell University I had been preparing myself to be a college professor of English. My first job after I received my Ph.D. in June 1941 was at Williams, an excellent and prestigious small college set in the mountains of western Massachusetts. The future looked bright, especially as viewed from the Berkshires.

The war arrived on 7 December 1941, and the circumstances in which it made itself known seemed to epitomize my life at Williams. In the company of three other faculty members, all of whom later became distinguished scholars in their fields, I had climbed a nearby Berkshire hill, Round Top. We had scrambled up

17

through the pines and birches, grasping the tree trunks to keep from sliding in the first snow of the young winter. At the crest we had wolfed down rare roast beef sandwiches while marveling at the loveliness of the New England countryside spread below us. Descending, we galloped and shouted down the mountainside, gasping in the crystalline air. We rollicked into Hallett Smith's living room where Betty Smith told us in a shocked voice that the New York Philharmonic Symphony broadcast had been interrupted by the announcement that the Japanese had attacked Pearl Harbor.

During the next three years I stayed on at Williams and taught air navigation to Navy V-5 aviation cadets. This was my contribution to the war and as useful a one as I could make, it seemed to me. But as 1944 drew to a close the Navy had trained all the flyers it could use, and the V-5 program began to phase out. Even though the Navy had enough pilots, the war gave no sign of ending. Some gloomy thinkers were predicting war for another ten years. I began casting about for some way to get actively involved. Then I learned that my English Department colleague, Roy Lamson, whom the war had transformed into Major Lamson and made the head of the historical staff of Army G-2, desperately needed people who could perform research and write history. He was certain I could be useful, and he invited me down to Washington for interviews.

On a frosty morning in February 1945 I boarded a train in North Adams, Massachusetts, waving goodbye to my wife, Rosemary, and my two-year-old son. As I sat in the dining car, keeping a wary eye on my surging coffee while the train ambled and swayed through the snowy meadows of the Hoosic Valley, my state of mind was that of a man departing on a special mission of short duration. I did not expect the war to last another ten years (neither did I expect it to be over in six or eight months), and I expected to return to my chosen profession, teaching.

The next morning I was at the Pentagon, filling out forms, being interviewed, and drinking lots of coffee. Shortly before noon Roy Lamson told me that a snag had developed. A colonel from Army personnel had discovered that Roy's staff contained fewer people with Ph.D.'s in history than it did in literature or other effete disciplines (by a tally of three to seven, in fact). This offended the colonel's notion of how a history unit should be staffed, so he ruled that no more nonhistory Ph.D.'s could be hired for the time being. To save my expedition from utter futility, Roy and his editorial assistant, Marjorie Cline (Mrs. Ray S. Cline), lined up interviews for me in the Office of Strategic Services (OSS) and the Board of Economic Warfare.

My first interview in OSS was with a man who spoke the same language as I, a professor of American literature. We had a promising but noncommittal discussion. But the next session was with the personnel director of the Board of Economic Warfare, a bureaucrat down to his toes in outlook, manner, and speech. Most especially, speech. I was thoroughly intimidated. He began with a twenty-minute account of his own career, offered, he told me sternly, "so that you will have confidence in my advice." It was a proud history whose theme seemed to be that each time President Franklin D. Roosevelt had felt the need to establish a new agency he had turned to my interlocutor to undertake the really essential task, selecting the personnel. At last he turned with what seemed considerable reluctance to me. "My purpose here is to channel your thinking. Just channel your thinking. Tell me, now, what your education has been."

I brightened at this. No problem here. I recounted the public schools in Dayton, Ohio, the A.B. at Miami University, and with a modest smile, the Ph.D. in English literature from Cornell. He did not seem impressed. In fact, he seemed saddened. He shook his head slowly, sorrowfully. "Well," he said, "it's difficult to see what use that could be to the United States Government, isn't it?"

I admitted that no particular use came immediately to mind. We looked at each other for a moment, and then he seemed almost to shake himself, determined to make something out of this deplorable situation. "Now let's see. Tell me what your experience has been."

I braced myself for a new try. Lumping together my years of labor as a filling station attendant, a movie theater usher, and deckhand on a Great Lakes ore freighter, I said I had held a

19

number of odd jobs but that for the past eight years I had been teaching English at Cornell University and Williams College. Thud. He looked at me despairingly and again shook his head. "It's very hard to see what use *that* could be to the U.S. government, isn't it?" He could see from the expression on my face that it beat the hell out of me. "Well," he said bravely, "tell you what we'll do. You fill out a half dozen of these personnel forms, and I'll shop them around. But I'll warn you, I'm not sanguine. Not at all *sanguine.*"

I took his proffered forms and slunk out the door. Outside on E Street, it was five o'clock of a darkening Saturday afternoon in February. I had one more appointment, one with Marjorie Cline's husband, Ray. I wavered for several minutes between keeping the appointment and slinking back to the Lamsons' where I knew the comfort of a cold martini and bright conversation awaited me. But I decided that I could not face Roy without keeping the date he had made for me, so I reluctantly made my way down to 2430 E Street. It was a fateful decision.

Two armed guards consulted visitors' lists and waved me through the guarded doors of the OSS presentation room. Ray Cline sat alone behind a handsome desk in a spectacularly beautiful room, one designed by Eero Saarinen, later architect of one of America's most distinctively beautiful buildings, Dulles Air Terminal. The room was the scene for top-level OSS briefings, and behind the richly handsome draperies along the walls were floor-to-ceiling sliding panels bearing highly classified maps and charts. Ray Cline, a chunky blond young man about my age, greeted me kindly and asked me to sit down.

His office was the presentation room, he explained, because he was chief of the current intelligence staff and among his responsibilities was maintaining the war maps and presenting briefings. Then he described his other duties, which included the publication of a daily intelligence bulletin and pamphlets on selected current topics. It was on these pamphlets that Ray placed most emphasis. He called them "current intelligence studies," and he described their preparation as being similar to an academic monograph. "We maintain high scholarly standards," he said. In fact, the activity of Ray's staff, as he described it, sounded very much like the publications unit of a large university press. It sounded good to me.

"Well," said Ray, "tell me what your educational background has been." Somewhat warily I went over Dayton public schools, Miami University, and a Cornell Ph.D. "Good," said Ray. "You've demonstrated that you know how to do research. I've found that people who can do research in one field can do it in another when they have familiarized themselves with the materials."

He smiled approvingly. "What has your experience been?" Heartened but cautious, I spoke of my eight years of teaching at Cornell and at Williams. Again Ray said, "Good. With that experience you ought to know how to present whatever your research turns up. Sounds to me as though you are just the kind of man we are looking for." Well, I thought to myself, that's more like it and allowed myself a broad smile. Ray and I spent another fifteen minutes on procedural details, and then I went to the Lamsons' for a victory martini.

Two months later I was back in Ray Cline's handsome office, security-cleared and a duly sworn OSS officer. I had traded the studious quiet of Williams for the brisk urgencies of a U.S. government agency at war. I had left the ancient trees and mountain-circled vistas of Williamstown for the asphalt pavements and nondescript buildings of Washington's Foggy Bottom. But I had no sense of loss. Instead, I felt lifted and exhilarated, part of something momentous. Washington at war was a heady, exciting place. It was easy to understand why war as an institution has survived despite its ravages and horrors. Except for those who are getting bombed or shot or made homeless, war bestows as many pleasures as it does pain. People's lives are given a significance they may previously have lacked, whether it be found in raising a victory garden, buying war bonds, making bandages, knitting socks, or working in a defense factory. War enhances the bond of national

21

unity and forges a sense of joined purpose. This was certainly true of Washington in early 1945. The city seemed filled with talented, articulate people who had left Manhattan law offices, Chicago and Detroit executive suites, or college campuses the country over. There was zest and energy in their manner and their talk.

The current intelligence staff of OSS held in small compass a representative sample of wartime people. We ranged from three mint-new Radcliffe graduates through a professional music critic, a brace of college teachers, and a radio broadcast newsman to a draft-captured senior editor of *Reader's Digest*. The Radcliffe girls were female counterparts of Williams students, prettier to my eye to be sure and in one instance, at least, possessed of a spectacularly handsome bosom. The two most attractive people, however, were the *Reader's Digest* editor, Maurice Ragsdale, and the radio newsman, Merritt Ruddock.

Ragsdale, it developed, was a surprise, a "sleeper." At first glance, he seemed a shy, gentle, almost formless man who had trouble speaking a straightforward sentence. His manner and appearance did nothing to dispel my well-nurtured prejudice against *Reader's Digest*. Like many young academics of my generation, I revered the *New Republic* and the *New Yorker* and cherished the James Thurber reply to a query about his regard for *Reader's Digest:* "Do you like bouillon cubes?" As it happened, my first assignment was to work as a staff man on the daily intelligence bulletin, of which Ragsdale was the editor. I began with considerable nonchalance, having great confidence in my ability to produce precise, expository writing. I had been the editor of my college newspaper, as well as my high school paper and two other school papers reaching back to the sixth grade, and I had taught freshman English composition for eight years. I turned in my first piece to Ragsdale, an item on the outbreak of jaundice in southern Italy, with professional—or at least semiprofessional—pride. The item was done up with a slugged all-cap head, short crisp paragraphs, and was finished off with the mandatory "-30-." I expected automatic approval. Instead, when he had finished reading it, Ragsdale began jabbing at the sheet with his pencil while seeming to grope for words. I peered over his shoulder at the spot he was pointing at and found to my chagrin an inexact referent. Worse, he found two other places where precision was absent. It was chastening. Over the next few weeks I acquired great respect for Maurice Ragsdale's prowess as an editor. He sometimes struck me as overfastidious, but he was never wrong. His eye was unerring in locating infirm timber in an English sentence.

Merritt Ruddock was a constant surprise and a delight. Six-feet-four with a hawk-like nose and deep-set piercing blue eyes, he attacked life with boundless zest and an unremitting playfulness. When Ray Cline introduced me, Ruddock was sitting at his massively cluttered desk furiously scrubbing and polishing his newly acquired second lieutenant's bar. He polished the insignia four or five times a day, he explained owlishly, in the hope that its color would change to that of a first lieutenant's bar. When he opened his desk drawer to put the polish away the inside looked like a jumble at a notions store. Shoestrings, Hershey bars, buttons, tie clips, Kleenex, and other oddments of Western civilization were crammed there. The next day, when Ruddock returned from his twice-weekly expedition to a nearby military PX, the desk drawer became understandable. He ambled into the office carrying a paper bag reaching up to his chin. Inside were more Hershey bars and more shoestrings, which he dispensed around the office like Santa Claus. He was the office wheeler-dealer, as the current Washington phrase had it. Anything that was hard to get in wartime Washington, Ruddock knew how to get.

But his skill as an operator extended beyond material acquisition; he was resourceful in dozens of ways. Looking for an apartment to house my wife and son, I asked him about the location of a Connecticut Avenue address I had found in a classified ad. "Don't know but let's find out," he said. He picked up a Yellow Pages classified directory, turned to the listing for a drugstore chain, ran his finger down until he found a Connecticut Avenue address reasonably close, and telephoned the store. "What's the nearest cross street to you?" Then he fished a map out of that jumble of treasure in his drawer and showed me where it was.

On our way to lunch that day we took a shortcut through one of the OSS buildings, and a guard tried to stop us. "You can't come into this building with that badge." Ruddock proceeded onward for another stride or two and then turned back. He pulled himself up straight and looked at least seven feet tall. "Our unit has not received that information, officer," he said looking down his chin at the man below, "but when it does you can rest assured we will obey it." The guard was reduced to mumbling something about not doing it again. As we walked down the narrow hallway, Ruddock whispered to me, "We're not supposed to know that this is where they keep all the counterfeiters and safecrackers." As we proceeded out of the building and down the street toward Rich's restaurant with its famous cheese blintzes, Ruddock suddenly wheeled around and went back to a parking meter that was displaying a red "Violation" tag beside a battered Chevrolet. He fished in his pocket for a nickel and pushed it into the meter. "This is what I call my 'casting bread upon the waters,' " he explained. He did this twice more before we reached Rich's.

But Ruddock was not only a delightful person; he was also a talented reporter. After graduation from Harvard he had worked on newspapers in Richmond, Virginia, and had moved on to radio broadcasting. He had had a nationwide one o'clock Mutual news slot before the war. He wrote reports with great facility and flair, his fingers flying as he punched out copy on an old Underwood typewriter. He had a fund of information in his head and a great knack for finding the pungent word and telling phrase. I did not realize it at the time, but the affection I developed for Ruddock and the respect I had for his talents were later to be instrumental in shaping my career.

After two weeks of apprenticeship under Ragsdale, Ray Cline assigned me the job of writing current intelligence studies on Japan. We were well into April 1945, and VE Day had come and gone. All energies were now focused against the Japanese. Current intelligence studies were the little research pamphlets Cline had mentioned in our first conversation. They were produced by the current intelligence staff after picking the brains and files of the analysts in the Research and Analysis Branch, a process that those people regarded as a nuisance and an intrusion. Moreover, it seemed, sexual antagonism had inflamed these normal reactions since Cline's forces were the Radcliffe girls and the R&A analysts also were young women. Without saying so, Ray made it clear that my status as a young male would probably be as important in successfully carrying out the assignment as my skills in research. He urged me to be as charming as possible. Actually, the two female ogres who were the R&A Japanese desk analysts turned out to be two highly professional, dedicated, and serious scholars, and I found that ordinary courtesy and a little professional deference (highly deserved given my painful state of ignorance) soon made them generous collaborators. They pointed me in the right direction on my first research paper, a study of the organization and methods of the Japanese secret police, the *Kempei-tai*. They found books and reports on the subject and opened their files to me. How much influence, if any, my status as a male had in this collaboration I was never able to determine. But I did perceive that Jane, one of the analysts, was a very agreeable young woman with a delightful sprinkling of little freckles across the bridge of her small nose, and I feel confident she was aware of my perception.

I finished the pamphlet in about a week. As I did, I realized that it contained remarkably little "secret" information, none of the juicy stuff spies are supposed to ferret out. Except for a detail or two from U.S. Army attaché reports, it could have been written by a graduate student working in his university library. But when Cline called me in to give me my next assignment he told me that the study had been especially well received by our readers. I put that down to the intrinsic fascination we all find in spies and secret police and to the likelihood that the readers were as poorly informed about things Japanese as I.

My next task was to do a study of the raison d'être of the Japanese Greater East Asia Co-prosperity Sphere, a peculiarly Japanese version of a Marshall Plan for the Asian countries the

Japanese then occupied. This turned out to be lots of fun, largely because most of the information we had on the subject came from Japanese radio propaganda, and I became fascinated in trying to discern grains of truth among tons of blather. It was obvious the Japanese were not broadcasting unvarnished truth in their English-language programs, and equally clear they were not telling flat-out lies. Reality, certain to be there if only in shadow, lay between. The first temptation was to guess that truth was the opposite of what was being said. Later, with the help of a few bits and pieces of agent reports and several hours of reading analytic studies, I came to believe that truth was to be discerned through something like prismatic *refraction*, not mirror-like reflection. With this technique I came up with a few insights. I found the whole endeavor exciting and satisfying. I later realized that in my first month in OSS I had come upon an undeviating constant of intelligence work: it is intellectually challenging and fun.

Indeed, I was finding the whole experience good fun. Washington in the summer of 1945 was exhilarating. The European Axis powers had been defeated, and General MacArthur's forces were advancing steadily and triumphantly up the Pacific Island chain. The streets of the city were dotted with military uniforms, and the sweet smell of victory was in the air. The people I met at cocktail parties were enthusiastic and happy in their work, most of them convinced that they were involved in a useful and winning cause. At dinner parties the conversation often turned to the postwar world, and agreement was general that the United States would have to nurse the grievously wounded British and French back to health and in the meantime assume the leadership of the Western world. To live in Washington in 1945 was to know that your country was great and powerful and good, possessed of the material and moral strength to lead the world into a new era of peace and good will.

As the summer wore on I found myself weighing the possibility of staying on in Washington instead of returning to teaching. This was unsettling because I had first dreamed of becoming a college teacher when I was a freshman at Miami University and had sustained that vision through college and four years of graduate school. The question came up one night after dinner in Merritt Ruddock's little Georgetown garden. My dinner companion asked me about my future plans, and I replied that I was weighing the possibility of staying in government. "Don't do it," she said. "Go back to the academic life. My husband's father is still teaching, and I don't know a happier man. You'll stay young longer in a college town."

As it happened I did not need to make a decision whether to go or stay. It was made for me. In early August came Hiroshima and the prompt Japanese surrender. Washington streets were filled with singing and shouting crowds on V-J Day and the joyous night that followed. The long war was over. And so, it seemed, was OSS. Ray Cline assembled us one afternoon in the handsome room and told us that the future looked very dark. Efforts had been under way for several months to obtain presidential backing for a peacetime central intelligence organization modeled after OSS, but so far there had been no progress. Hope was not dead, however. Even as he talked there was a plan afoot to arouse Bess Truman's interest in the hope she would persuade the president. (I was a novice on the Washington scene, but even then that seemed to me an extremely dubious maneuver.) In any event, there was no need for panic; our jobs would be secure for some months to come, but we should recognize that we were in a phasing-out situation. We would be wise to look about for other employment and certainly well advised to consider seriously anything offered.

I thought the matter over for the next few days. I realized that prospects were poor for a return to college teaching that autumn. It was already the last week of August, and teaching rosters were certainly filled for the fall semester. I did not have academic tenure at Williams and could not hope to return there until student enrollments climbed back to normal levels. Perhaps the best thing was to look around Washington for a job to sustain me until I could return to the academic world. Through friends I made some interviews at the Department of State. I took along my handful of OSS studies on Japan. The State people were polite—barely—but they left no uncertainty about their low regard for my expertise on Japan. They were right.

The next week I got an unexpected long-distance telephone call from William C. DeVane in New Haven, Connecticut. DeVane had been chairman of the Cornell English Department and my graduate adviser when I had gone to Cornell in 1937. Now he was dean of Yale College and also a member of the Wells College board of trustees.

There had been a last-minute departure from the Wells College English Department, and the department needed someone immediately to teach courses in the seventeenth century and in literary criticism. DeVane knew that these were my special interests and wished to recommend me for the post. If I was at all interested, I was to interview with Colonel Richard Armour then working in the Pentagon.

I knew a little about Wells College at Aurora on Cayuga Lake, just twenty-five miles north of Ithaca, from my four years at Cornell. It had a lovely campus, with handsome trees and a lawn sloping down to the shore of Aurora Bay. It was a woman's college, founded by Henry Wells of Wells-Fargo and American Express in emulation of his friend, Ezra Cornell. Its academic reputation was excellent. I went to the Pentagon to see Richard Armour, who turned out to be the writer of these bright little jingles and poems I had been reading for years on the editorial page of the *Saturday Evening Post* and the *Saturday Review*. He was on leave from Wells. We had a pleasant and successful interview, and I made some modest stipulations about salary and rank. Armour called me the next day to tell me that my stipulations were acceptable and that the college wanted me to report within three days. Classes began the following week.

Rosemary and I frantically loaded our old Plymouth with books, records, and the family dog and set out for the Finger Lakes Country. The first morning in Aurora I left the Aurora Inn after breakfast and walked two blocks north to the edge of the village. Below me Cayuga Lake spangled and rippled in the soft morning breeze. Just beyond a fence several cows cropped grass in a meadow that stretched far up the hill to a grove of pine trees. It was a little after eight o'clock. At that same moment, I knew, the L-5 and L-20 buses were spouting diesel exhaust while rushing full loads of government workers into central Washington. Typewriters would start to click and telephones to ring. I suddenly felt content. I had done the right thing. I was right to come back to the academic life and its quiet pleasures. But though I did not know it then, a part of me was not convinced.

I had worked only six months in OSS, not enough time even to learn my own job well, let alone the intelligence business. But somehow, in that time a small seed was planted, and it was only a matter of time before its growth would make me restless.

The next two years at Wells College, however, were idyllic. We lived in a 1795 house with generous rooms and enormous fireplaces in the simple village of Aurora. From our windows Cayuga Lake spread a blue splendor before us. There was duck hunting and goose hunting in the fall with my neighbor across the street, Eliot Lauderdale, a lover of life's hearty pleasures. There was golf, swimming, and sailing in spring and summer. My students ranged from good to excellent, and my elective courses were well attended. I could probably have stayed on at Wells until retirement, and if I had become discontented at Wells I could probably have published my way free to another college or university. While writing my doctoral dissertation at Cornell I had come upon an unworked vein of rich ore regarding John Dryden, the dominant figure in late seventeenth-century English literature. I had some things to say that had previously been unsaid about Dryden, and I was looking forward to saying them. Why, then, did my mind keep wandering back to Washington?

The front pages of the *New York Times* were the proximate cause. A succession of events marked the initial skirmishing of the Cold War in 1945–46, and then Hungary fell under communist rule in the elections of 1946. Also on the front pages were stories about the establishment of a national intelligence authority and the Central Intelligence Group (CIG) under Admiral Sidney Souers. International affairs had an immediacy and urgency for me that they had never held before. Coupled with this new level of interest was the knowledge I had acquired in OSS that I had skills that could be useful in dealing with international problems. For the first time I began to wonder whether I had not been born fifty years too late to devote myself to a lifetime of teaching seventeenth-century English poetry at a small college for young ladies. I loved teaching English literature; I valued intensely the insights and perspectives that came to me through the pressures of the classroom. I was living a good and abundant life. But still. . . .

I decided to vent my restlessness, or at least to soothe my curiousity, by asking Ray Cline what he thought about these new developments, particularly the Central Intelligence Group. A prompt reply from Ray told me he knew relatively little about the new organization. He had left OSS shortly after I had and was working in the Pentagon, writing the wartime history of the Army's operations division, a work that was subsequently published as *Washington Command Post* and won Ray both distinction and a Ph.D. from Harvard. He told me that Merritt Ruddock had emerged as chief of the current intelligence staff in the CIG, and he was sure Merritt would respond to my inquiry.

Respond Ruddock certainly did. His letter offered me a job as his deputy at an estimated salary roughly two and a half times my academic pay, and in customary Ruddock fashion he followed this letter with a telegram setting a date in Washington for a job interview. It did not take me long to decide. I found that my mind was more settled than I had realized about leaving teaching, and my resistance to returning to Washington was minimal. The decision was made even easier by the fact that I would be working with Merritt Ruddock. I knew the standards of performance would be high and the atmosphere never stuffy.

Early Years

I entered on duty with CIG on 26 June 1947 and joined Ruddock in his second floor office in M Building, a paper-thin wartime temporary building squatting beside the turreted Heurich Brewery. I found Ruddock in a hyperactive state, a charged, eye-snapping tempo that I soon took to calling his "overdrive" when I wanted to calm him down. He had been single-handedly putting out the current intelligence summary six days a week for nearly six months. Unlike its OSS predecessor, which performed for an uncertain audience, the CIG daily intelligence summary had a specific, receptive reader, President Harry Truman. When CIG was first being organized, Truman began asking almost daily, "Where's my newspaper?" It seemed almost that the only CIG activity President Truman deemed important was the daily summary. Putting out this high-level publication was a high-speed operation with an inflexible deadline. To add to the strain, Ruddock had been accomplishing this daily feat in the midst of an organizational chaos that made his operation resemble that of a circus wild-animal trainer working without benefit of cage, chair, or whip.

It was a classic instance of authority to command not matching the responsibility to perform. The Central Intelligence Group, then only six months old, consisted mostly of hastily assembled analysts possessing varying levels of expertise regarding countries of the world. They were organized into geographic, regional branches. Each branch was headed by a senior officer who occupied—and here was the glitch—a status exactly equal to that of the editor of the daily summary. This resulted in daily confrontations between the editor and the chief of one or more geographic branches over the choice of items to be published, a battle that usually revolved around the question, "Is this important enough to be brought to President Truman's attention?"

Now, experts in any field are a most peculiar breed. To a person they suffer from professional myopia. Steeped in the minutiae of their field, in this instance the daily flow of events in a country, they frequently mistake back-page filler items for front-page, ban-

31

ner-headline stories. Moreover, they have a persistent tendency to believe that their sometimes arcane thought processes will be transparent to their reader.

My favorite example of this is the reply given me one time by a Latin American specialist. We were looking over some graphics he had prepared for inclusion in a piece on oil production in Central America. One graphic was a map of the region. The map was traversed by a wandering dotted red line, the legend for which was "Impassible Route." "Wait a minute," I said. "What's an 'impassible route?' That's a contradiction in terms."

"Oh," he said airily, as though speaking to a backward child, "that's the proposed route of the Pan-American Highway."

"Oh, well," I said in relief. "In that case let's just change the legend to 'Proposed Pan-American Highway.'"

"What?" he asked indignantly, "And not tell all our readers you can't possibly put a road down through that terrain?"

With one or two exceptions, the geographic branch chiefs were not truly regional experts, but they all sustained a healthy respect for their own bureaucratic status. Besides, they had their stable of experts to respond to. If Mr. Jones with a Ph.D. from South Central State said the latest little blip from Paraguay was significant, the chief was willing to fight and die on his behalf. One day a representative from the Latin American section showed up at my desk with a report that hoof-and-mouth disease had been discovered among cattle being shipped from the United States to Guatemala. I looked up at him wonderingly. "I don't get it. What's significant about that?" The Latin American expert smirked. "My chief thinks it's terribly important." I answered that its meaning continued to escape me. "Don't you see? The United States takes a tough line against South American beef because of the hoof-and-mouth problem, and now it turns out *we* are sending diseased cattle down there."

"Pretty cute. But I still don't think President Truman needs to be told about it." I sent the piece back.

Ten minutes later the Latin American chief came striding in, hair and arms flying, gray herringbone jacket and flannel slacks proclaiming his status as a fugitive Ivy League professor. "I understand you had a little trouble understanding this item. I've written a short comment that will explain it to the most untutored." I took the paper and read his comment. It was a supercilious, smart-alecky statement that would have insulted every reader, including the president of the United States.

And so the battle was joined. My adversary's tactic was to cite his superior knowledge of the Latin American scene; I was to take his word for it: it was important. I rebutted that it fell short of presidential significance. Useful, perhaps, to a Department of State or Department of Commerce assistant secretary but not worthy of the beleaguered attention of the president. He then turned our bureaucratic pas de deux into a jurisdictional waltz. By the authority vested in him as chief of the Latin American branch it was his right to determine what intelligence was important south of the border. My move was that I was responsible for making the daily intelligence summary worthy of the president's attention. As I was speaking, my eye fell on a misspelled word in the piece. "I can do this job either of two ways," I said. "I can make the best judgment I can about selecting items, or I can spend my time correcting the misspellings in your pieces." I circled the errant word.

He looked as though he had been slapped. He snatched the paper from my desk, crumpling it as he stalked out of the office. "Wreaths of fire!" he exclaimed and raised his hands high as he strode out the door.

That was just another day in the life of the editor of President Truman's newspaper, a job I took over from Ruddock shortly after my arrival. It was not always necessary to be snide; sometimes we won through Ruddock's favorite tactic: "Let's hold it until tomorrow. Maybe we'll get something more on it." "Tomorrow" it would be too stale to print. But either way it was a struggle, an unnecessary struggle that wasted time and energy. And the cause was a simple organizational flaw: responsibility and authority did not match.

The comic backdrop to this daily turmoil was that in actuality *nobody* knew what President Truman wanted to see or not see. And of course there was an added kicker in that I, fresh from the Finger Lakes village of Aurora and the maidenly quiet of English Lit. 20, should be presuming to decide. I had tried as I sat beside Merritt Ruddock during the first morning—between an endless succession of telephone calls, a lovely string of dirty stories, and some virtuoso doodling—to establish for myself criteria for selecting the material. How were we supposed to judge, sitting in a run-down temporary building on the edge of the Potomac, what was fit for the president's eyes? It became apparent there were no established criteria. No one in the White House had told the Central Intelligence Group what was important for the president to see. This startled me considerably, but I later came to recognize it as a persistent problem in the relationship between intelligence people and people who make policy. Rarely is there guidance. The process is usually carried out by feel, one of the reasons intelligence work is often termed an art.

With no guideposts at hand I began modeling my set of values on Ruddock's intuition. I began to understand as I gained experience that intelligence of immediate value to the president falls essentially into two categories: developments impinging directly on the security of the United States; and developments bearing on major U.S. policy concerns. These cover possible military attacks, fluctuations in relationships among potential adversaries, or anything likely to threaten or enhance the success of major U.S. policy programs worldwide.

In those dim early days CIA's intelligence-gathering abilities were not likely to cause lights to burn late at night in the White House. Military intelligence had phased down sharply after 1945, and espionage nets were primitive. Sophisticated overhead photography was still a decade away, and communications intelligence (the deciphering of coded messages) was denied us for direct use, even in the publication for the president. Top people were permitted to see the intercepts in a vaulted room, and occasionally we received warnings not to accept certain reports that were belied by such an intercept. One of those warnings was delivered to Ruddock my first day. A short man with a dark mustache slipped up to the desk wearing, I noted, gum-soled shoes. He leaned over until his face was about ten inches from Ruddock's and spoke a rapid-fire sentence. Ruddock nodded, and the small man turned on his gum soles and slipped out. I had not heard a word he said although I was only a foot away, and I was terribly impressed. What I had just witnessed, I was certain, was genuine professional clandestinity. I said to Ruddock in genuine amazement, "That's really something! I didn't hear a word that man said to you."

Ruddock leaned back confidentially. "You know something? I didn't either!" And he slapped his knee and wiped his hand across his face as he guffawed.

But despite the relatively low level of our intelligence material, we were involved in reporting matters more vital than hoof-and-mouth disease in Guatemala or the impossibility of building the Pan-American Highway down the proposed route. These were the dawning days of the Cold War, and the Soviet Union was daily becoming more truculent and uncooperative. There was still alive in Washington a sentiment that we should have taken on the Soviets and finished the job in Europe while we still had a magnificent army in the field. A very considerable segment of official Washington spoke frequently of the "Russian timetable for world domination" and expressed the view that the only real question was *when* the Soviet armies would launch their attack and sweep across Europe. Against this backdrop of tense expectation, the Soviets steadily tightened their hold on Eastern Europe and the Soviet sector of Berlin.

Prior to the Berlin blockade and the building of the Berlin wall, there was a succession of provocative moves. Each time a U.S. convoy was halted on the autobahn by a Soviet official, the fledging analytic forces in CIG felt compelled to provide an analysis of the significance of the move and its portent. In truth we seldom had any facts other than that the closure of the Berlin corridor had been announced, and our "informed" speculation was also a slender thing. The chief of the Soviet section was a personable Virginian who had served during World War II as a U.S. liaison officer with the Soviets in Murmansk. He had developed an appropriate cynicism regarding Soviet intentions but made no claim to being a serious student of Soviet affairs. His assistant, a regular Army colonel, given to frequent explosions of expletives in a high-pitched voice, had served in intelligence in the European theater. The level of Soviet expertise then current in CIG perhaps can be measured by a reply the treble-voiced colonel gave me when I stopped him one day as he was rushing down the hall waving a sheaf of cables. We were trying to get a special evaluation of the latest Soviet obstruction down to the White House by noon, and I asked him how he was coming. *"Christ!"* he shrilled. "I don't know the answer. I've got *six* reasons why they did it, and the chief's got *seven.* And none of them agrees with each other!"

Still, we felt obliged to give the White House the best judgment we could command, and we continued to try as the years passed by. Eventually, as it developed, the cumulative experience of this persistent effort, combined with the recruitment of some genuine specialists and scholars, produced a level of expertise that had no counterpart elsewhere in the government. But this was a decade or more away.

The first major international crisis after my return to Washington occurred in the spring of 1948. It was a lovely Saturday morning in April, and it was Ruddock's turn to put out the summary. I was laying plans for a leisurely day when the phone rang. "I think you'd better come in," said Merritt, and he refused to say more. When I arrived, reluctant and grumpy, he was holding court to an office full of chattering people, waving his arms and clearly enjoying the hell out of it. "It's Bogotá," he said. "Rioting and burning, all communications cut off, and we can't locate the secretary of state or any of the American delegates to the Inter-American Conference." In my mood this seemed quite unworld-shaking, so I said, "Is that all?"

Ruddock looked at me in disbelief. "This is pretty great stuff. I didn't want you to miss it." Waspishly I asked what there was to do. "Here's all we've got," he said handing me a small sheaf of cables, "and we're trying to get a special evaluation over to the White House before twelve noon." I took the messages and withdrew from the hubbub into another office. With the help of a Latin American editorial assistant, a quiet, effective man, I pieced together what we knew. A protest demonstration had taken place, and the leader of the opposition, Jorge Gaitan, had been assassinated. The demonstration itself was not surprising because political ferment was bubbling in Colombia, but the degree of violence was unexpected. Our information suggested it was spontaneous, not planned.

I put a piece together and went back to Ruddock's office, where a free-form discussion still swirled, and laid it before him. He looked up in surprise. "I must say I admire your professional calm." I did not tell him that my cool was mostly annoyance. I could not share the joyous exuberance of Ruddock and the other people in the office. Somehow I found it unnecessary and even silly. I later learned that I had this reaction every time there was a crisis. It apparently was a deep-seated temperamental trait and not merely the result of temporary irritation that morning. Other people with whom I worked during my career complimented me at times on my professional poise during flaps. I never confessed that really I only wanted to get things under control. Looking back, I think now that I was the loser in those situations. Left to himself, Merritt Ruddock would have beaten the deadline—but just barely—with an incisive, elegant account and would have had a whale of a time doing it. Our styles were different; his probably better. Or at least more fun.

There later emerged a valuable lesson from the Bogotá affair that I never forgot. Subsequent newspaper accounts quoted Secretary of State George C. Marshall, who along with the other American delegates was unharmed, as saying the rioting was a communist-directed effort to discredit the Colombian government and disrupt the Inter-American Conference. This presented the Agency with its first intelligence "failure." Over the next day or two, I reviewed all the messages we had received prior to the outbreak, and our reconstruction was that the demonstration had flared spontaneously and that the communists had sought to exploit the disturbances after they had begun. Puzzled, I telephoned my opposite number in the secretary's secretariat in the State Department. "Where did the secretary get the information that the rioting in Bogotá was a communist plot?" "Oh," he said casually, "he just looked out of the window in his villa six or seven miles away and said, 'The communists did it.' "

This was my first, and best, lesson on the difference between a diplomatic public statement and an intelligence assessment. The secretary of state was not making an intelligence judgment. He was making an operational statement whose purpose was to save face for the Colombian government. That they did not coincide was no great problem except to congressional right-wingers who called our director, Admiral Roscoe Hillenkoetter, before them to explain this lack of foresight regarding a communist plot. The clandestine services flushed out of the system a few reports of dubious reliability in a misguided effort to prove that we had information in advance. But no one could make the case that the information was hard enough to give firm warning to the secretary and the delegation. My own judgment remained that communist involvement consisted of some attempts to take advantage of a spontaneous disturbance.

Slightly more than a year after my return to Washington, Merritt Ruddock left the current intelligence staff to join Frank Wisner's new covert action unit, the Office of Policy Coordination. We were the Central Intelligence Agency then, established by the National Security Act of September 1947. Wisner's group was the covert action arm that U.S. leadership deemed essential in meeting the Soviet Cold War thrust. With Ruddock's departure I was promoted to chief of current intelligence and in immediate need of a deputy to assist me.

I had been impressed by W. Osborn Webb who was chief of the Eastern European section. Obbie, educated at Groton and Yale, came from an old, distinguished New York family. He wrote well, with an easy, transparent style that transmitted information effortlessly, and he had an endlessly curious mind. I have never known anyone with a more highly developed intellectual curiosity, and his questions always were genuine, not designed to advance a thesis. Most of all I liked Obbie's manner: quiet, smooth, and unflappable. He never seemed hurried and never raised his voice. I felt that our styles would mesh effectively. Obbie agreed to join me, and he and I worked in close harmony for the next fifteen years.

Another professional relationship that was to have significance for my career was established about this time—more accurately, resumed—with Ray Cline. Late in the spring of 1949 Ray invited me over to the Pentagon for lunch. He was finishing up his history project, he told me, and wanted my views on the advisability of staying in Washington or returning to the academic world. Midway through the discussion I realized that Ray was gently letting me know he was available for a return to intelligence work. After lunch I went directly to Ludwell Montague, chief of the Global Survey Group, and urged him to hire Ray. It took little urging; Montague had known Cline during the war and promptly hired him for his staff. I was pleased I had been able to repay Ray for hiring me that grim Saturday afternoon in 1945. Apparently, it also strengthened a mutual regard that later had considerable consequence for me.

Osborn Webb and I soon had the current intelligence operation running smoothly. The experts continued to balk from time to time at our cavalier treatment of their prized pieces, but as time wore on they seemed increasingly willing to bow, no matter how reluctantly. Meanwhile, as my professional life encountered these oc-

39

casional frustrations intermixed with moments of genuine excitement and achievement, my personal life reveled in the ambiance of the nation's capital. Washington was delightful and exhilarating in the late forties. Sometimes in the spring and fall, my wife, Rosemary, would pack a picnic lunch, and we would sit on the bank of the Potomac, one hundred feet from my office, and watch the graceful three-tailed Constellations glide overhead on their way into National Airport. Other times we lunched at the Watergate Restaurant whose windows commanded a view of Theodore Roosevelt Island, and sometimes we ate at Aldo's Restaurant beneath a grape arbor with ripe grapes hanging temptingly above our heads. Occasionally we enjoyed the fruits of Chesapeake Bay at the waterfront places beside the fish wharves. We saw good theater at the National Theater. For music, we had WGMS classical broadcasts and the National Symphony concerts at Constitution Hall. Baseball held unchallenged dominance on the American sport scene in the late 1940s, and Washington still had a major league team. I could take my young son to Griffith Stadium, a fine, old-fashioned ballpark, where in exchange for the ineptitudes of the Washington Senators we could admire the professional skills of the New York Yankees and the fluid grace of Joe Dimaggio. Each morning brought the *Washington Post*, which was, before success inflated its pretensions and self-esteem, a lean, zestful newspaper with youthful, liberal views, its pages enhanced by Herblock, Shirley Povich, Stewart and Joseph Alsop, and Walter Lippman.

Washington was a lovely city with long, graceful vistas: the cascading cherry blossoms in the spring, Mr. Lincoln brooding serenely in his chair overlooking the Mall, Mr. Jefferson standing elegantly beside the Tidal Basin, the Washington Monument, like a mountain peak, changing its aspect with every shift of light. But above all it was a proud city, peopled by proud government servants. Our government was a good government with high purpose. The war had left our European friends exhausted, and it was up to us to take over their responsibilities in the world. We were strong, free from inhibiting tradition; we knew how to attack problems and how to solve them. Our people were intelligent and idealistic. We did not want to extend our dominion abroad; we wanted merely to help less fortunate people everywhere. The communists under Soviet direction were seeking to thwart our purposes, but our Marshall Plan was effectively reducing their field of maneuver, and the Truman Doctrine supporting the resistance in Greece was succeeding. From Washington in the late 1940s the world looked challenging but manageable.

But as the 1940s came to an end, and 1949 gave way to 1950, a growing restlessness began to prevail in my corner of CIA. Slowly the realization had grown that there had to be a better way to produce high-level intelligence for our national leaders. Despite our best efforts our reports and studies lacked true authority. We began to perceive the shortcomings.

They began with the quality of our raw information. A national intelligence organization, a *central intelligence agency*—which we were by force of the National Security Act of 1947—must be provided with all the intelligence on international affairs the government possesses. We were not. Our best flow of information came from the Department of State, a broad array of cables including highly sensitive reports seen only by top people in State. Indeed, my State colleagues occasionally pointed out to me that our daily intelligence summary was essentially a digest of top State telegrams. Military intelligence was markedly inferior, consisting of weekly reports from military attachés and reports of naval visits to foreign ports. Missing were the high-level messages of top military commanders overseas giving their assessments of local developments.

But what was most seriously lacking, aside from intercepted ciphers as I have already mentioned, were good clandestine reports. The publications of a national intelligence organization ought to be heavily enriched by secret information from spies or technical espionage. This is the essential ingredient; it is what people expect to find in CIA-published reports. Ours lacked them. The reason, I discovered later, was that the best clandestine reports were being hand-carried by top clandestine services people over to senior people in the White House, the State Department, and the Pentagon. On reflection, the rationale was clear. CIA clandestine operations require assistance from departments with facilities overseas. High-quality espionage reports form a *quid* of a quid pro quo, not only good business but samples of the return to be anticipated from new clandestine ventures. By contrast to these choice tidbits, the reports we saw were mostly inconsequential scraps of information about foreign personalities, especially the officers of local communist cells. Knowing nothing about espionage except what had been divulged in the pages of Joseph Conrad and Rudyard Kipling, and being more than a little naive, I assumed that what I saw was the best American espionage could produce. It was several years before I learned better. Meanwhile, the clandestine services of CIA were to an extent thwarting the purposes of their parent organization without, I suppose, being aware of it.

The shortcomings extended beyond an inadequate flow of sensitive information. We were not fulfilling our primary task of combining Pentagon, State Department, and CIA judgments into national intelligence estimates. The system, born of the blasts and scars of Pearl Harbor, was not working. This had been mercilessly pointed out in the Jackson-Correa Report of 1948. We had all expected a great shake-up after the anticipated triumph of Governor Thomas Dewey in the election of 1948. But Harry Truman took care of that threat; little or nothing was done to implement the recommendations of Jackson-Correa; we bumbled along in 1949 and early 1950 much as before.

To say it succinctly, CIA lacked clout. The military and diplomatic people ignored our statutory authority in these matters, and the CIA leadership lacked the power to compel compliance. Our director was Rear Admiral Roscoe Hillenkoetter, a thoroughly decent, unpretentious man, but a rear admiral. In the hierarchical maze of official Washington his authority scarcely extended beyond the front door. Hillenkoetter's low rank precisely indicated the level of enthusiasm the rank-conscious armed services had for a centralized intelligence system.

But change came in the wake of the Korean War, which burst upon us in the late spring of 1950 and disclosed glaring inadequacies. In the inevitable congressional investigation that followed the "CIA failure" to predict the North Korean attack, it became clear that several subsidiary groups in Washington had foreseen it, but no national intelligence estimate had lifted its strong voice in warning. The "surprise" made it evident that the work of creating a national intelligence system was incomplete. This realization, combined with the ominous possibility, vividly urgent in the minds of many Americans, that the attack in Korea signaled a communist leap from political pressure to military action that presaged World War III, jarred the White House into action. Within a short time the appointment of General Walter Bedell Smith as director of CIA was announced, an event that not only alerted all intelligence people in the U.S. government that serious work was about to begin, but also brought to the task a man of genuine brilliance, great personal force, and organizational genius.

The Beedle Smith Era

3

General Walter Bedell Smith, "Beedle" to military colleagues, was not one of the dashing field generals of World War II. No Omar Bradley or George Patton, he was nonetheless a man of tremendous power in SHAEF, Supreme Headquarters Allied Expeditionary Forces. He was General Eisenhower's chief of staff, and there he had gained his reputation as an exacting, hard-hitting executive who brooked neither mediocrity nor ineptitude, a man who not only barked but bit. Besides his role as hatchet man for the seemingly mild-mannered Ike, we knew only that he had begun his military career as an enlisted man and worked his way up through the ranks to lieutenant general. That fact alone made him seem formidable. As I left the office of the soon-departing Admiral Hillenkoetter, after bringing him some sensitive cables to read on his last day, he shook my hand in his courteous way and said, "Goodbye, Jack. I hope we'll be shipmates again sometime." Things around here, I thought to myself, will soon be very different.

I first met General Smith unexpectedly in an incident that I thought fleetingly might end my CIA career. The first national estimate done under Beedle Smith's command, a set of analyses of Far Eastern problems, was being prepared especially for President Truman prior to his meeting with General Douglas MacArthur on Wake Island. The drafting of these papers had been done by Ludwell Montague, and their final coordination had been accomplished at an afternoon meeting of military and State Department intelligence chiefs under Beedle Smith's chairmanship. It was well past six and dark outside my office windows when Montague turned the texts over to me for printing. They were due at the White House next morning. "The general says to get them out as fast as you can."

"We're all set to run." Montague left, and I began to perform a final light editing before turning them over to the printer. In a few minutes I hit a snag. In one of the key, estimative sentences there was a wide-open ambiguity. The sentence as written could mean A or it could mean Z. Nothing in between and no context to give clues as to whether it was really A or Z. What to do? The estimate could not be printed and sent to President Truman like that. I tried to call Montague. No answer. I called the director's office. "I need to talk to someone who was present at the meeting this afternoon. There's something here I can't understand."

"Wait a second." I could hear muffled voices through the cupped hand over the mouthpiece. "Come on up. Bill Jackson's still here." Jackson, a New York lawyer and World War II intelligence officer, was Bedell Smith's deputy. I had met him once and had swiftly gained the impression that in his view all of us who worked in CIA prior to the new team's arrival were misguided dolts. Still, he had been at the meeting.

I crossed the dark alley between M Building and Heurich's Brewery and climbed the wooden stair and walkway alongside South Building. I found Bill Jackson standing in the outer office. Before him, slumped in a chair, a brown fedora hat down over his eyes, sat a slender man I did not recognize. "Oh, here," said Jackson when he saw me, "come in my office, and we'll look at this."

46

The man in the chair spoke from under his hat. "What's this?" I looked again as he straightened up. It was Bedell Smith, an extremely thin version of the broad-jawed man who had been pictured on front pages accepting the surrender of the German generals. Extensive surgery for ulcers had stripped him of forty pounds.

"Oh, Smith here has some problem with the paper we did this afternoon. I'm going to straighten it out."

General Smith sat up erect. "What is it? Let me see."

I took the paper out of the envelope and walked over to him. I opened to the troublesome page. "I can't understand this penciled-in part, sir."

He squinted at the page where my finger pointed and said, "The hell you can't. I printed it so you could."

I squatted down beside his chair, still holding the paper. "Oh, I can read it all right, but I still don't know just what it means."

The general looked again. "Well, it also happens that I wrote that sentence myself." This was said with a general's bark.

"I think it's all right, General," offered Jackson.

With dimming courage I pressed on. "Well, sir, let me show you what I mean." Using my finger to point to the various parts of the sentence, I said, "I don't know whether this refers to this, or to that."

The general took the paper out of my hands. "I see." He turned then to Jackson. "He says the antecedent here isn't the subject of the sentence. He's an *editor*." He spoke the word with an emphasis that seemed to consign all editors to the outer rings of hell. He turned back to the page and read it again. "I don't see why that isn't perfectly clear as it stands." He read it aloud, giving it as he did an emphasis and inflection that revealed its intended meaning. He shoved the paper back to me. "That sentence means just what it says."

"Why, sure, General," said Jackson. "It's perfectly clear."

47

I took a very deep breath. "All right, sir, but if I misread it the first time I saw it, someone else may misread it also. I think it can be made to say exactly what you want it to say."

The silence that followed was prolonged and weighted. Bedell Smith looked at me with great intensity. Then he spoke, very softly. "This is a good boy." He looked at me again, but his gaze had lost a little of its rigor. "All right, then. How would you fix it?"

I straightened up with relief. "Now that I know what it's supposed to mean I can fix it easily."

He reached for the paper in my hand. "No, you fix it right here so I can see it before you take it away." I squatted down again beside him and, using the general's thigh as a desktop, penciled in a conjunction and a comma that brought clarity. When I finished, Bedell Smith smiled. "That's fine. That's a good job," he said to Jackson. Turning back to me, he said, "You keep up the good work and in the future don't hesitate to make any changes like that. You make any you think are necessary. You have carte blanche."

William Jackson chuckled. "Now don't spoil the boy, General. Don't spoil him."

To keep from tugging at my forelock, I reminded myself that I was thirty-seven years old, the holder of a Cornell Ph.D., and the father of an eight-year-old. I thanked General Smith for his kindness and trudged off into the night. Next day Beedle's secretary told me that the general had growled that "Montague and Smith" were the only people around CIA doing any useful work.

My participation in the Wake Island estimates was my first involvement with the soon-to-be created Office of National Estimates (ONE). Bedell Smith's first act had been to call for the creation of this high-level group that would report directly to him and would perform CIA's number one task, the production of coordinated national intelligence estimates. He set about this characteristically by telephoning Dr. William Langer at Harvard, saying he wanted to talk with him. Assuming that Bedell Smith wanted some advice

48

based on his experience as chief of research and analysis in OSS, Langer agreed to come down for a talk. "Fine," said Bedell. "I'll send my airplane up for you the first clear day." In his CIA office, General Smith told Langer he wanted him to set up and run the new Office of National Estimates.

"Oh, thank you, General," said Langer in his North Boston twang. "I'm flattered by your offer, but I've just got back to full-time teaching after a nine-year leave of absence from Harvard, and I——"

General Smith broke in. "Dr. Langer, you have no choice. The president asked me to come down here in this national emergency, and I am unable to think of anyone else who can do this important job."

Describing the interview later, the distinguished Harvard historian said with resignation, "What can you say to a fella like that? He was ordered down here by the president, and he brought only half his stomach with him!"

Ray Cline told this story over lunch with Osborn Webb and me. After his meeting with Beedle Smith, Langer had asked Ray for his assistance recruiting a small staff of analysts for the new office. Ray had pointed out that because of his fairly recent arrival at CIA he did not know the personnel very well, and he recommended Osborn Webb and me as "fellows who did." Cline suggested we assemble a roster of top-flight regional experts to present to Dr. Langer.

After lunch, Obbie and I went out in the nearby park and tried to put together a list of the best and brightest regional people in the office. It turned out to be a surprisingly short list. Back in the building I walked up and down the corridor, peering in office doorways to see if I had missed someone likely. The next day I took my list up the wooden steps alongside South Building to meet Dr. Langer. I found him in one of the corner offices, trim, spare, dark-suited, looking exactly like a senior college professor. Beside him was Sherman Kent, his creased mastiff-like face seemingly exhibiting all the signs of a massive hangover. Langer addressed me with his one-in-a-million voice, somewhere between a nasal twang and a whine: "Ray tells me you know some fellas who can come up here and help us out on these estimates." I said I did. "Well, what we want, Jack,"—he drew my name out in a long, falling cadence—"is some fellas who can look over the cables as they come in and keep us up to date. Maybe a half-dozen fellas." I expressed concern over the small number, but Langer was firm. His concept was that the new office, ONE, would consist of a board and a staff. The board would be composed of ten or twelve senior people—academics, lawyers, military officers, business executives—and the staff would have about an equal number of younger men—regional experts and generalists. The basic text of the estimates would be prepared by intelligence agencies in the Pentagon and the State Department, pulled together into a composite whole by the generalists with the assistance of the regional experts who would update their information, and then reviewed by the board for soundness of judgment. The estimate would be passed then to the director of central intelligence who, if he approved of it, would assemble the chiefs of the departmental intelligence agencies and obtain their joint approval. This layered gestation would culminate in a national intelligence estimate (NIE).

It was a well-structured, beautiful concept with no more than the usual number of unrealistic assumptions and misconceptions. I will point these out as we move along, but first, you may ask, what were these estimates to be about? The quick answer: international situations likely to affect the nation's security significantly. More specifically, the rumblings and maneuvers of the Soviet Union, the truculent enigma of Communist China and the closely linked future of Nationalist China, political instability in France and Italy, the wash of the Soviet tide against Greece, the future of Egypt, India, and a host of lesser former colonies in Africa and Southeast Asia set adrift in the wake of Great Britain's departure, and the communist advance in Vietnam. There was ample grist for the new mill in serving American leadership as it sought to deal with the tumbling problems of the postwar world.

In those early days, those of us already at work before the new wave of people brought down to Washington by Beedle Smith and William Jackson endured more than one bruising encounter. It was my first experience with institutional reformers, and it was a most instructive one. The new crowd of New York and Boston lawyers, bankers, and investment counselors, most of whom had had some intelligence or military staff experience in World War II, had a running start at moral superiority because they had been pulled out of their lucrative peacetime occupations to assist in a national emergency. The urgent rhetoric of Beedle Smith and events in East Europe and Korea had convinced them that their country was once again in peril, probably sliding rapidly into World War III, and their presence was essential for the nation's survival. Besides, they had been told, quite correctly, that the national intelligence organization was a mess. They would set it right. So convinced were they of their superior understanding of the business that they spurned all suggestions from us. But to us their professional expertise was not immediately overpowering.

Shortly after I joined Dr. Langer, he took me to a session devoted to organizing the new Office of Current Intelligence. An investment banker from New York was the newly appointed chief of OCI. "How are things going?" asked William Jackson, who was presiding over the meeting.

"All right," said the banker. "I've got one thing straightened out so far. I've stopped all the subscriptions to the *New York Times*. You walk down the halls at nine o'clock in the morning, and in every office you see nothing but people reading the *Times*. So I've cut that out as of today."

Jackson nodded approvingly, but Langer was not about to stifle his unceasing flow of common sense in the interests of mere civility. "But, Bi-l-l-l-l," he said in a long, curving whine, "there's a lot of good stuff in the *New York Times*. A lot of good informa-a-a-tion."

The *New York Times*, an essential tool to intelligence analysts because of its thorough world coverage, was restored to OCI in a

51

short time, and the banker eventually made an effective contribution to the new organization. But, as I say, the initial impression did not always convey professionalism.

I finally came to the conclusion that the new team members resembled all reformers. It was necessary for them to feel an overpowering sense of rightness, that they held truth in their grasp and must impress it upon the lost souls they found floundering in Washington. They had all been summoned to CIA by an imperious, hand-picked general whose overriding sense of mission conveyed to them the exhilarating idea that they were being rushed to the front to combat a national emergency. Without the conviction that they alone knew the right path, they would have had little to bring and might better have stayed in their New York offices.

In any event, it eventually all worked out and for the most part worked out well. Bedell Smith was a man of intense convictions but not, as he demonstrated with me that November night, unreasonable. He could recognize a good idea even when it was not his own, and he set the tone for the place. As it worked out, those professionals who genuinely had judgment and talent won the respect of the newcomers, and those newcomers who could contribute solidly stayed at least for the duration of General Smith's regime, and the others left shortly with his blessing.

In the new Office of National Estimates there was a minimum of jostling between professionals and newcomers. Langer's good sense, as cold and as penetrating as a wind off the North Atlantic, and his disdain for pomp and pretense made it all but impossible. The distinguished men he had selected for the Board reflected his good judgment. Sherman Kent, ex-Yale historian and author of a recent book on strategic intelligence, was as down-to-earth as chewing tobacco. Raymond Sontag, ex-Princeton historian, had specialized in German political affairs and brought penetrating judgment to bear on European postwar developments. Calvin Hoover, ex-Duke University economist, leavened his very considerable knowledge of economics with common-sense judgment. Max Foster, a New York lawyer of William Jackson's acquaintance, wore a brown fedora hat at all our meetings, but besides this eccentricity, he demonstrated a capacity for searching insight.

The staff was about fifteen years younger on the average but among its number were several who later attained fame greater than most of the board. Ray Cline, Harvard Ph.D. and Balliol College Fellow, later became director of State Department intelligence and still later director of studies at the Georgetown University Center for Strategic and International Studies. Chester Cooper held several White House senior staff posts and wrote two highly acclaimed books, *The Lion's Last Roar*, on Britain's 1956 Suez adventure, and *The Lost Crusade*, on Vietnam. Robert Komer became a valued aide to President Lyndon Johnson, won both fame and "blowtorch" opprobium as head of American pacification programs in Vietnam, was rewarded by President Johnson with the ambassadorship to Turkey, and became deputy secretary of defense under President Carter.

Very early in ONE a highly charged relationship grew up between staff and board. The differing responsibilities of the two groups—the staff wrote the draft estimates, the board revised them—provided a seedbed for rivalry. Like all serious and intense young men, the staff had a strong tendency to rebel against the authority of the board, while the older men, mostly senior professors accustomed to dealing authoritatively with graduate students, expected their judgment to prevail. Langer would have none of it. In one of the first meetings, Ray Cline took sharp issue with Ray Sontag, a clash that was inevitable given Sontag's occasional tendency toward prima donna attitudes and Cline's disdain for nonrational argument. When challenged, Sontag sought to prevail by claiming the superior rank of a board member. Langer intervened. "But Ra-a-a-a-y. A young fellow can have a good idea too, don'tcha kno-o-o-w." That set the tone. The daily discussions that took place about the latest maneuver by the Soviets or the murky scene in China were marked by intellectual rough-and-tumble of a high order. Needless to say, the staff adored Dr. Langer and accepted without dismay his blunt criticism. His orderly, uncluttered mind favored directness above all things, and he detested wooliness and wordiness. He expressed this, as always, directly. "There are too many words in these sentences, fellas. Just wo-o-o-ords!" Without cavil, the staff set to work revising.

No job I ever had in the intelligence business was more challenging and satisfying than writing the first draft of a national intelligence estimate. Let's say the subject was "Likelihood of Imminent Arab-Israeli War." Before you on your desk would be assembled all the intelligence the United States possessed on that subject, consisting of military attaché reports on the relative strengths of the opposing forces, U.S. Embassy analyses of concerns and goals of the rival governments, and agent reports of unusual military preparations and troop movements. These you would put together in a coherent account, fifteen to twenty-five pages long, that would tell your reader how things stood at present, what further developments would signal the imminent onset of war, and your best judgment as to when the tensions would boil over. Some of these pronouncements would rest on very thin ice. There is almost never enough firm intelligence to support a solid, definitive statement. If there were, there would be no need for an estimate; the threat would be self-evident. So, writing an estimate required some risk-taking, some chasm-jumping, and this was part of the challenge. The satisfying part came when your leaps across the unknown were accepted by your peers and superiors and presented to the president of the United States as the official position of the Central Intelligence Agency.

After the satisfactions of assembling and crafting a draft national intelligence estimate, the CIA staff officer had to endure stabs of pain as his draft passed through a prolonged review gauntlet. The first leg was a review by the Board of National Estimates. These were lively occasions, marked by barbed exchanges. The staff often felt that the changes made in their carefully wrought papers were capricious and possibly malicious. There was a grain of truth here in that the board, seemingly by implicit assent, tolerated the personal crotchets of each other. For instance,

Ray Sontag, the ex-Princeton professor, once took sharp exception to my use of the word "limited," as in "The Indonesian government's success in quelling the guerrilla operations has been *limited.*" "The word doesn't mean anything," he proclaimed. Puzzled, I asked why. The professor drew himself up erect, his narrow, aristocratic face stern as Moses, "Because *everything* is limited under God!" A sound theological point, I said inwardly, but a poor semantic one. I changed "limited" to "slight."

Actually, these frictions were no more than the side effects of serious work by high-quality people. After the smoke had blown away, the staff officer would almost invariably discover that the main frame of his paper, and many of his best touches, had survived intact. Most of the damage consisted of nicks and scratches around the edges.

But then came the coordination meetings with the State Department and Pentagon intelligence agencies, a far more harrowing stage. "Coordination" carries a wide range of meaning within the government, but as applied to national intelligence estimates it was supposed to ensure that all the facts available to American intelligence agencies were accurately reported and that the judgments made—for example, "Neither Arab nor Israeli forces will be able to complete preparations for attack for at least six months"—were sound and shared by all. Instead, these meetings consisted of an incredibly minute examination, sentence by sentence, hour by hour, word by word, day after day, comma by comma. Few people are able to separate an idea or judgment from the particular phrasing in which it is couched and to discuss the *idea* not its phrasing. For example, in the sentence quoted, a U.S. Army major might opine that military preparations are never really complete, and he cannot "buy" that idea. Forty minutes of palaver might ensue before changing "complete preparations to attack" to "ready preparations" and so on. The Army major might "buy" that only to hear his U.S. Navy colleague beside him object that "at least six months" sounds "like it is too long. That 'at least.' I mean it could be just *about* six months." More extended palaver, and the phrase is changed to "about six months or so." Everyone is now convinced, except the original drafter, that "Neither Arab nor Israeli Forces will be able to *ready* preparations for attack for *about* six months *or so*" is better than the original. No one seems to realize that most readers, especially harried readers like presidents and secretaries of state, would skim through either version and come out with the same thought: "We have about six months before anything is likely to happen."

Occasionally, *very* occasionally, a truly major change in the judgment was made, but it was about as rare as orange blossoms in the Yukon. Mostly it was an unbelievable waste of time and energy, its only virtue being that it usually persuaded the State Department and Pentagon representatives that they had participated in forming a national intelligence estimate. They had "coordinated."

By contrast, the final stage of this gauntlet was short and sweet. Especially under the incisive chairmanship of Beedle Smith. At one of the first meetings of the assembled chiefs of military and State Department intelligence agencies, the U.S. Intelligence Board, the Army G-2 raised a minor, verbal objection. Unfortunately, the G-2 was a mere major general—let's call him "Alexander Blank"—who had served under General Smith as a colonel. General Smith looked down the table at him, a slight smile on his thin lips, "Now, little Alex," he said, "you're not going to delay us with nit-picks like that, are you?" The G-2 guessed not, and the meeting sped on to a rapid conclusion.

The final word in the production of national intelligence estimates was not always accompanied by such a display of military muscle, but it was usually brief, sometimes almost perfunctory. The real work had been done by the staff of ONE and to a lesser extent by the board. I often wished that Beedle Smith could be persuaded to take over one of those interminable coordination meetings for just long enough to put the fear of those gleaming three stars in the hearts of the captains and majors from the Pentagon.

Academic Interlude

4

The Office of National Estimates was organized in late 1950. By the spring of 1951 the initial confusions had been resolved and an organizational arrangement worked out. The staff was divided into a General Group and geographic specialists, two or three to a region. Osborn Webb and I by this time had turned over the daily and weekly publications to the new Office of Current Intelligence and were members of the General Group. Before I could get very involved in estimates work, however, Dr. Langer offered me a new and exciting prospect. Bedell Smith had asked him to name a candidate for the National War College, a ten-month course beginning in August. "It's a pretty good thing, Ja-a-a-ck. I think you might like it."

I knew very well I would like it. An assignment to the National War College was a great privilege. It was the nation's graduate school for national strategy. The men who were selected were expected to rise to leadership in the armed services, the State Department, and related government agencies. My classmates would be the Bedell Smiths of my generation. Located at Fort McNair on a spur of land between the Anacostia River and the Washington Channel, the National War College was ensconced in the handsome old building of the Army War College designed by Stanford White about 1900. It possessed a fine library and offered daily lectures by distinguished men from all fields. Moreover, it offered almost a full year's relief from the daily push and a chance to recharge my intellectual batteries.

I did not hesitate in accepting Dr. Langer's offer. In late August I walked through the impressive entrance of Stanford White's building and registered as a member of the Class of 1952. In a military-operated school I had expected a certain amount of military clanking and bureaucratic stuffiness, so I was a little taken aback by the administrative and academic freedom that permeated the place. I soon appreciated that this sprang from the influence of one man, its commandant, Lieutenant General Harold Rowe Bull, a somewhat short and somewhat round man whose red hair and crimson cheeks had long ago won him the nickname "Pinky." Pinky Bull was one of General George C. Marshall's men, part of the remarkable team Marshall put together to run the U.S. Army in World War II. Bull became General Eisenhower's G-3 in SHAEF. He had left a farm in Vermont for West Point, and somehow his career in the Army had shaped a man of broad tolerance and understanding, gentleness, and true thoughtfulness.

"All year long the discussion will go on," said General Bull as he addressed the NWC Class of 1952 on opening day. "In the car pools in the morning and evening, in the committee rooms, over lunch, and at your class parties. By the way, speaking of lunch: you don't need to sign in or out, but you might make a notation of your destination on the daily register in case there is some unexpected emergency at home like a burst pipe. But meanwhile, keep the discussion going. Try out your own ideas; listen to the other fellows. There are no 'school solutions' here. We'll accept any idea at all, so long as it's a good one."

The day's study at the National War College began with a lecture at nine o'clock. All the heavy-duty strategists of the time spoke during the course of the year: Dean Acheson, Lieutenant General Albert C. Wedemeyer, Charles Bohlen, George Kennan, Philip Jessup. In addition, there was a steady parade of public figures and academic stars: Gordon Dean, chairman of the Atomic Energy Commission; Vannevar Bush of the Massachusetts Institute of Technology (MIT); Margaret Mead, the anthropologist; Senator John S. Sparkman of Alabama; K. T. Keller, president of Chrysler Corporation.

After the lecture, lasting usually about an hour, came a question period that occasionally ran on until noon. The questions were sometimes breezy, often irreverent, but usually pointed and searching. Some of my classmates found the question period a tempting opportunity to state their own convictions on the subject. For example, Charlton Ogburn, who later wrote several compelling books on natural conservation, then a member of the State Department, found this occasion irresistibly alluring. Several times, after a long eloquent discourse that ventured close to being a harangue, he would stop suddenly and say, "I think there's a question mark in there somewhere."

General Bull tolerated such flippancies with calm, good humor, but he would not permit rudeness or ill humor. If a class member got too sharp, Bull would get out of his front row seat quickly and take charge. "I wonder if we could rephrase that question. Perhaps this is what you would like to ask. . . ." He was just as firm in handling the visitors. If a speaker flipped aside a good and pertinent question, Bull would rise and ask if he might pose a question. Then he would say a sentence or two about the importance of the matter under discussion and the value the group attached to the speaker's judgment. Then he would gently phrase the question in his own terms. I never saw a speaker refuse to take the jump.

Only General Curtis LeMay, the "terrible tempered Mr. Bang" who was then chief of the Strategic Air Command (SAC), got away with a sharp retort. He was being questioned about the security of the bomber fleet from surprise attack. After admitting that the bombers were "out there, parked wingtip to wingtip" because airfield space was inadequate, he was asked a follow-on question that he seemed to feel contained a needle. He drew his powerful figure up. "If you are asking me, sir, whether SAC knows how to do its job, the answer is, 'You're goddammed right!' " The class roared with laughter, and the discussion moved on.

Dean Acheson spoke to us early in the course, on a Thursday a week before the Japanese Peace Treaty talks, an occasion of great triumph for him as secretary of state. I found him impressive and decided then to keep an informal journal to record my reactions to our distinguished speakers. Of Acheson, I wrote:

> I was struck by the massive command and control he has of his information, the views he holds, his articulation of them. He cited two key errors in strategic thought: one, the "perfect answer," which is thought to exist for every problem if only we think long and hard enough. (He said there are no perfect answers, just some not as bad as others); and the other, the "key log in the jam" theory, which suggests that if we solve the key problem with the USSR everything else will fall in place (he thinks instead we must work relentlessly and patiently toward some adjustment, bit by bit). He is popularly considered cold and arrogant—I instead thought him deeply emotional but checked and reined by high standards of thought and conduct.

It was on this appearance that Acheson made a response I later used many times when I myself was a speaker. When a student prefaced his statement with an apology for an "indiscreet" question, Dean Acheson interrupted him with a courtly flourish: "Please forgive me, sir, if I seem to correct you by suggesting that there are no indiscreet questions. There are only indiscreet answers."

Acheson was followed sometime later by George Kennan who was then head of the State Department Policy Planning Staff, well known as the author of the famous "Mr. X" article in *Foreign*

Affairs that articulated the Truman Doctrine for containing the Soviets. He was also announced appointee as ambassador to the USSR. I found him one of the most interesting speakers of the year and commented in my journal:

> The specific point he made that impressed me was that the Soviet system suffers from crystallization and immobility at the top of the government structure. No provision seems to exist at present for introducing new blood into the organism, and no means of exit seems to exist except the undertaker. A telling point with many implications.
>
> As a man, Kennan impresses one with his precision of statement and his undogmatic argumentation . . . essentially an academic mind—objective, detached, tentative, and humble. My State classmates tell me that this is a false impression— an aura that K. projects from the platform that does not otherwise exist. They say he is essentially a prima donna— intellectually arrogant, rigid, and intolerant. They say also that he has reduced his effectiveness in the department to a rel- atively low status by his inability to give and take in an exchange of ideas.

Of course, not all of our speakers were American diplomats. We also heard Sir Oliver Franks, then British ambassador to the United States, a tall, ruddy-faced man with the air of an English don, who impressed me as "an honest good-hearted man, rising bravely, doggedly, and good-humoredly to answer one hard question after another." When he finished with one particularly engaging sally, the class gave him a standing ovation—the only one all year. Another Britisher was the First Sea Lord of the British Admiralty Sir Rhoderick McGregor, who delighted us by characterizing the Irish in the Royal Navy as "great people who love to fight and want to belong to the club without paying the dues." The broad reach of the course in national strategy also brought us such disparate national figures as Irving J. Brown, European representative of the American Federation of Labor; Elmer Davis, then dean of American news broadcasters; Eric Johnston, ex-Hollywood executive and director of the Economic Stabilization Agency; and Supreme Court Justice William O. Douglas, whom my notes characterized as "ostentatiously simple, speaking with the accent and unadorned diction of an educated Western farmer."

A most remarkable lecturer was Lieutenant General Anton von Bechtolsheim, who wowed the class with a lecture on "German Strategy against the USSR." I was almost as intrigued by the reactions of my military classmates, who listened attentively to this man who had been their enemy in battle only a few years before, as I was by the general himself. His theme was simple, almost predictable: without Hitler's interference in military strategy, the Soviets could not have defeated the Germans. But he detailed and buttressed his case most impressively in a ninety-minute lecture. Throughout he was, as I recorded in my journal,

> a beautifully schooled professional soldier. The contrast between his expertise and the fumbling discourse of the U.S. strategists we have heard recently was painful. He was an honest-to-God professional. And yet, overlaying this gleaming technical competence was a rich Germanic flavoring. In an outline of his talk, which was issued beforehand and was complete even to a detailed eight-page chronography, he used such Wagnerian devices as, "Act I of Tragedy: Extravagant Hopes;" and "Act V of Tragedy: Final Agony and Disaster." He was treated with real respect by the military, and he deserved to be. He was possessed of a certain ironic sense of humor, and he mingled a kind of at-your-service quality with a quiet and solid pride. It was a matter of: we were beaten, yes, but we know why we were beaten, and the margin of defeat was not only not great but could have been eliminated if the pros had run the show.

When we were not attending lectures or seminars, I found myself admiring the building and grounds of the college. Stanford White's turn-of-the-century building is a graceful brick-and-stone structure standing imposingly at the end of a long parade ground that runs almost unbroken to the front gate. What breaks this long sweep are two low brick buildings, built shortly before the Civil War, one of which held Mary Surratt, an accomplice in President Lincoln's assassination, until her trial and subsequent hanging on the present tennis courts of the post. According to an oft-told story, Stanford White stipulated that these buildings be removed so that his handsome facade would unimpeded greet the eye of the visitor as he turned in the gate. The Army agreed but later could not find the heart to destroy three solid, useful structures. When White came down by train from New York to inspect his creation, he took a carriage from Union Station. As the horses turned into the entrance and White looked expectantly toward the planned vista, his eye met the squat red buildings midway on the parade ground. Legend has it that he ordered the carriage turned around, and he returned to New York without ever inspecting his new building.

Inside, the War College building displays marble floors and a foyer three stories high, rising past circular balconies to a great dome. But the library is the prize. It, too, rises three stories, with the stacks of bookshelves forming the side walls. At the south end of the room is a large bay, with deep leather chairs before the leaded glass windows. I spent many happy and fruitful hours reading in those chairs.

The eastern half of the former parade ground has been made into a small golf course, virtually a pitch and putt. General Bull made it clear at the outset of the year that we were expected to spend an hour to an hour and a half daily in physical exercise. There was swimming at a large pool on the post, squash and handball in the basement of the building, sailboating at the nearby Corinthian Yacht Club, baseball, and, of course, golf. We were encouraged to sign up for one or more of these sports. I elected golf and sailing.

The social life of the National War College class was intense. The college faculty organized three or four functions for the school year, and the class itself took the social initiative from there. A

Marine colonel, perhaps, had always wanted to have a long, gloves-off talk with an Army counterpart; or an Air Force fighter pilot had long wanted to discuss the intricacies of Navy carrier-borne aviation. Some of my classmates were curious as to what CIA was really like. Often these talks developed into friendships; we had much to learn from each other. Cocktails and dinner parties became the natural next step.

As a group, my military classmates were an attractive lot, vigorous, alert, articulate. From years spent in the semiformal social environment of peacetime military posts, they had become highly adept socially, and they all seemed skilled in a kind of humorous banter that seems peculiarly theirs and that I still find both engaging and impossible to imitate. I was especially impressed with a half-dozen or more of my Army colleagues who clearly possessed top-flight minds, which they used with a breadth and grace that I had previously observed only in academically trained people. Moreover, they had that indefinable but unmistakable quality of command—an assurance, an ease of manner that bespoke leadership. In later years I was pleased to find that my judgment was shared by the Army top command as several of these classmates rose to four-star general rank: Paul L. Freeman, Jr.; Andrew P. O'Meara; and James H. Polk, among others.

Among the State Department members, I found Robert McClintock the most impressive. Rob was a compact man who dressed impeccably and possessed a flashing wit. He could be a charming silken courtier or an arrogant martinet. In this latter role he infuriated and alienated a number of people, including my fellow CIA officers, but I saw very little of this side. Instead, I saw a superbly schooled diplomat, possessing the requisite skills in negotiation, languages, and knowledge of protocol. To one colleague who later characterized Rob as a son of a bitch, I replied, "Maybe, but you'll have to admit he's a *professional* son of a bitch."

To another I summed up McClintock's skills, "If you sent him in to an international negotiation to get an agreement, you could be positive he would come out with it in his hand."

Rob McClintock and I became good friends, and he awarded me the title of "Permanent First Mate" on his boat. At the start of the year, McClintock volunteered to organize the noon sailing activity. He returned from the nearby Corinthian Yacht Club, which owned a small fleet of Penguins—fourteen-foot racing dinghies— saying that the boats were not suitable for grown men. It was pointed out that previous NWC classes had used them successfully, but Rob was adamant. Not possible. Apparently there would be no sailing. Then, in what I later came to recognize as a typical McClintock recovery from a situation of his own making, he bought a used twenty-foot Herreshof day sailer and systematically began inviting all the men on the sailing roster, three at a time, to go sailing. By late November, I was the only guest sailor hardy, or foolhardy, enough to continue to accept. McClintock and I donned thermal underwear and ski mittens and, after making certain that a bottle of scotch was still stowed in the cuddy, pushed off from the Corinthian Yacht Club several times a week all during December, January, and February. In the raw wind whipping over the Anacostia and Potomac rivers a warm friendship was forged. Later, as Rob McClintock moved from one diplomatic post to another, and I traveled widely on CIA business, we sailed together in the warmer waters of the Tonle Sap in Cambodia, in the Mediterranean from Beirut to Byblos, and in the River Platte below Buenos Aires. After retirement we were planning a cruising venture in the Greek Isles when he was tragically and senselessly killed by a drunken driver in Beaune, France.

As the calendar turned the corner at the end of the year and headed toward spring my military colleagues grew visibly restless. They were awaiting the outcome of the Pentagon's annual assignment lottery that would determine the course of their careers. To a man they craved a post outside Washington—a training base in deep Texas or even a garrison in Alaska, anything to remove them from "that five-sided crazy house." They wanted a command just as my State Department colleagues all wanted their own embassy, a wish that only Rob McClintock had enough rank and seniority in 1952 to support realistically.

This restlessness soon infected me, so I invited Sherman Kent to lunch at the Fort McNair Officers' Club. Sherman was slated to replace William Langer when Langer returned to Harvard at the end of the year. Over lunch, Kent and I discussed my future.

"What we badly need, RJ," said Sherm, "is someone to mount a serious effort on Latin America. How would you like to become our house Latino?"

Latin America has never occupied a place in American foreign policy commensurate with its importance, but in 1952, with the Cold War at full blast, it had a status roughly comparable to Antarctica. To me, such an assignment looked denigrating. "I think it would be a fate worse than death," I told him.

One might expect the head of an office with the prestige of ONE to take a firm line with one of his officers, certainly to put on a little pressure, possibly even to insist. But that would not have been consonant with the academic freedom of ONE, and it certainly would not have been Sherman Kent's approach. He might grumble privately to someone later that he could not "get that mule-headed RJ to do a fucking thing," but he would not complain to me. The unwritten code of ONE seemed to be that one was expected to respond honorably and without pressure to a call to duty, and when one refused, an invisible black mark was entered in an invisible ledger. One day an accumulation of black marks would delay a promotion or deny you a desired assignment.

And so, Sherman Kent merely creased his face in an exaggerated grimace (all Sherman's gestures, like his language, tended toward hyperbole) and said to the white tablecloth between us, "Umm. Thought you'd say that. Well, then, how would you like to take over the Far East staff? Chet Cooper is coming here to the NWC next year."

That I would like. The Far East was full of ferment and interesting problems: the two Chinas, Japan, Vietnam, Indonesia, Malaya. "Great," I said. "I would like it."

"Good stuff!" said Sherman with customary vehemence. "You're on."

With next year's assignments known among my classmates, and the consequent period of exultation or despair over, all thoughts turned toward the thesis we were required to write before the end of the year. I wanted to use the opportunity to think through some fundamental problem about intelligence. At first I considered the use of estimative language; that is, how to convey to policy readers with maximum precision the judgments and findings of the intelligence people. I had been disturbed by this problem in ONE's estimates. At the sessions between the board and the ONE staff, and again during the interminable coordinating meetings with the intelligence agency representatives, there were long, sweaty debates over the exact meaning of a word or phrase conveying a key judgment. Satisfaction and resolution came in this process only when all present were agreed as to the exact significance of the debated word. As a former teacher of semantics I knew that this was hocus-pocus and mumbo-jumbo. A word is a mechanism that triggers responses within a reader's mind. It can mean no more than he takes it to mean. Unless the reader is present when the discussion takes place and can hear for himself the exact and weighted meaning intended in a given sentence, the long debate is irrelevant and futile. The reader will take the word in what he regards as its usual sense, modified and shaped by the surrounding context, and read on—unaware of any intent to invest the word with extraordinary meaning.

As I reflected, it came to me that the difficulty probably began with the academic background of the ruling spirits of ONE. Their writing had been directed toward monographs and scholarly essays. Sitting in the quiet of their book-lined offices they had as their potential readers only serious students and scholars like themselves. Being easily understood was a lesser value, ranked well below accuracy and fidelity to the evidence. As a group they had not written for a newspaper or confronted the rigors of a tough editorial pencil. The style of national estimates, I decided half-seriously, ought to be modeled on highway billboards for drivers moving at sixty-five miles an hour. Only that might approximate the fleeting attention we could expect from the president of the United States and his aides, who were besieged by the incredible pressures of national affairs.

After further thought I put aside the language of estimates as a thesis topic and turned to an even more fundamental matter: prediction in intelligence estimates. For most people both in and out of government, prediction is the name of the game. What's going to happen? It seems so proper a question, really the nub of intelligence work. But for an American leader it has significant limitations if only because every international problem is affected by the attitudes and actions of the United States. Unless you know what the United States intends to do in a crisis you cannot begin to predict how it will turn out. Henry Kissinger tried in the 1970s to address this difficulty by presenting intelligence with a set of optional courses of action to be analyzed for their impact on the outcome. It is a partial answer to the intelligence man's riposte, "Tell me what you plan to do, and I will try to tell you what will happen."

But as I worked my way toward a more fundamental solution, I came to the conclusion that national intelligence estimates could be most useful if they concentrated on analyzing the dynamics of an international situation—locating and describing its mainsprings and sources of tension—and less on its probable outcome. In writing my thesis, I called prediction an effort "to write history in advance," and I suggested that it would be better for the policy maker to understand what made an international problem tick, what its chief components were, and how they interacted. Ideally, he could be shown where the pressure points were in the situation and then, knowing the range of feasible U.S. actions, could select a policy that would exert pressure at the right place. To give a simple example, a U.S. trade embargo against a country vitally dependent upon U.S. trade might deflect a military adventure in the making.

It was not a great piece of work, but it helped me to clarify my thinking on an important aspect of my profession. I was flattered when one of my classmates, Jimmy Polk, who was assigned the following year to be an instructor at the Army War College in

Carlisle, Pennsylvania, had it reproduced and used as a text in the course.

With the graduation thesis out of the way we were free to turn our minds to the dessert at the NWC, a trip overseas. Up to that point my foreign travel had consisted of a two-hour peek at Tijuana and a twenty-minute stint of standing on Canadian soil while handling the hawser lines of an ore freighter southward bound through the Canadian side of the shipping locks at Sault Sainte Marie. I carefully masked my virginity in overseas travel from my classmates, nearly all of whom had served overseas, while I inspected the four trips offered: Far East, Latin America, Western Europe, and the Mediterranean. I chose the Mediterranean trip because it included stops at Paris and Rome as well as Athens and Ankara. The official purpose of the trip was to study the missions and tasks of the North Atlantic Treaty Organization in the area (NATO South), but my private purpose was to see as many foreign cities as possible.

Our group, led by General Bull, assembled at the Military Air Transport Service (MATS) terminal at Washington National Airport on a misty, foggy morning in late April and took off in two C-54s, the military equivalent of the four-engined DC-4. We stopped at Stephensville, Newfoundland, for dinner and at London Heathrow for breakfast. We arrived in Paris in midafternoon and by five o'clock were installed in our billets at the Crillon Hotel. Three of us shared a large suite with a bathroom as large as my living room at home. My roommates, a Navy captain and an Army colonel, both of them hardbitten, experienced travelers, got out a bottle of Old Grand-Dad bourbon and settled down to some serious drinking. To me this seemed sacrilege. Outside, the Place de la Concorde lay shimmering in the late afternoon sunlight while the graceful bridges arched over the Seine just beyond. I excused myself and left. Outside I met Colonel Albert ("Bub") Clark, later general and commandant of the Air Force Academy, and Bromley Smith, later presidential assistant for national security affairs. We strolled along the Seine, savored the soaring glories of Notre Dame and Sainte

Chappelles, drank "fine et l'eau" at the Deux Maggots boulevard cafe, ate dinner at a noisy student cafe Brom had known in his Parisian student days, and ended with a tour of night clubs at Place Pigalle. When I returned to the Crillon, my roommates told me that after punishing the Old Grand-Dad they ate "the best goddammed dinner in Paris," a $1 steak platter at the embassy cafeteria next door to the Crillon. I groaned.

As a serious study of NATO in the spring of 1952, our trip served mainly to convince my military colleagues that the obstacles to military efficiency of the organization were nearly insuperable. It began with the linguistic and communication difficulties of an internationally integrated command: a French officer commanding an American officer with a Belgian subordinate. Ray Murray, a big-shouldered Marine colonel from Texas, was most eloquent on the subject. Because of an ambiguity in the wording of the command for the order of march during the retreat from the Yalu River in the grim Korean winter of 1950, Ray had watched the heavy guns bog down in the slush and mire and bring the whole retreating column to a helpless halt. The heavy guns belonged at the tail of the column behind the troops and the light vehicles, but a slight imprecision had placed them at the head. Ray felt that such snarls would be endemic in a multilingual headquarters like Supreme Headquarters, Allied Powers, Europe (SHAPE).

The regard for NATO's military effectiveness reached rock bottom, however, during a briefing at the headquarters at Salzburg. The briefing colonel was asked what the U.S. Army detachment regarded as its first priority mission upon the outbreak of war. "To evacuate our dependents down the LOC [line of communication] to Leghorn, Italy," he said.

"How long is that LOC?" he was asked.

"About 400 miles."

My military classmates could scarcely contain their incredulity. "That's their first priority mission?" they asked each other derisively in the bus after the briefing. "We've got forces tied down out here whose chief purpose is to evacuate their own dependents?"

And so the group's opinion, after our sixteen-day swing through NATO South, was that NATO might have justifiable political values for the United States in the spring of 1952 but as a military instrument for countering Soviet aggression it was a facade, probably containing more liabilities than benefits. This was not a blindingly unique judgment, to be sure, but it had the benefit of on-the-ground inspection. For me, this aspect of our spring trip was most instructive and provided valuable background for future estimative work, but the novice European tourist in me was also wide-eyed and delighted by a succession of vignettes:

. . . the smartly groomed café-au-lait negress who caught my eye one midnight outside Hotel Crillon and, as I looked hastily away while passing, said in a low, tragic tone, *"Non?"*;

. . . riding around the Colosseum late at night, jammed with three other large-bottomed men in a high-fendered fiacre drawn by a bony little horse;

. . . breakfasting in my room at Hotel Vesuvius in Naples with my attention swinging from hard Italian rolls to the Castel del Ovo dreaming under my window in the soft early morning sunshine;

. . . the tax collector stationed in a small boat outside the Blue Grotto of Capri, who meticulously gave each of us a receipt before we glided through the low entrance into the vaulted cave where the water sprayed from the boatsman's oars in shimmering blue showers;

. . . walking down Attaturk Bulvari in Ankara in late afternoon, the clean, cool air laden with spring fragrance, feeling that I had reached the eastern edge of our civilization;

. . . finding it thoroughly impossible, at the Grande Bretagne Hotel in Athens, to get out of the way of Greek citizens who, on their way in and out of elevators, walked through me and over me but never around me;

71

. . . the Miramar Castle near Trieste where I stood on a stone balcony overlooking the sea, thinking of Carlotta and Maxmillian, and watched large fish swimming below me in the clear Mediterranean;

. . . walking down the narrow streets of Berchtesgaden, breathing the piney Alpine air at 5:30 in the morning, and meeting three of my classmates coming back from an even earlier walk;

. . . being greeted at dawn on the stark flats of Keflavik airport by a silver-blonde Icelandic hostess who was as breathcatchingly lovely as legend has it all Icelandic women are;

. . . the warm smiles of my wife and son who greeted me as we climbed wearily out of our C-54 at National Airport, Washington, in the late afternoon.

The War College course moved swiftly on to its close after the trip. Soon we were attending the graduation ceremonies where I found myself thinking that the year at the National War College was about the finest experience a government officer could have.

Looking back, what did it mean to me in my career as a professional intelligence officer? First, it gave me a chance to recharge my intellectual batteries. For five years after leaving the academic life I had been in high-pressure work. I had neither leisure nor energy for systematic reading. At NWC I had both, and my extensive reading, combined with the stimulus of the lectures and the hurly-burly discussions, had stocked my mind with new perceptions and insights. Second, I had seen firsthand most top leaders then in government; I had observed how their minds worked and had several times exchanged views with them directly. I felt I understood them. Third, I came away with a firm grasp of the qualities and essential characteristics of senior military men. I knew the main outlines of their value system, in particular their keen respect for clean delineation of authority. I enjoyed their company, and the fact that I "got on with the military" played a role in future assignments. Fourth, I made friends with a number of officers, both civilian and military, who rose to high rank in their respective organizations: a half-dozen ambassadors, a score or more of admirals and generals, and a presidential assistant or two. In later years when traveling overseas I was given access to the best information the embassy or command possessed, and briefings were easily arranged, including interviews with top foreign officials.

One of General Pinky Bull's intentions was to forge an "Old Boys' network" among National War College graduates. To this end he had wrested from his superiors the concession that all of us were made members of the Fort McNair Officers' Club where we could maintain our relationships after returning to our separate organizations. He succeeded. In years to come I could telephone and get help at lunch from Philip Barringer in the secretary of defense's office, Albert Gerhardt on the Joint Staff of the Joint Chiefs, Bromley Smith at the White House and the National Security Council, Christopher Merrillat at the Agency for International Development (AID), and so on. When they could not help directly, they could get the right person to call me. It was a valuable asset to me and to CIA.

The Watch on Asia

5

The Office of National Estimates I returned to in the summer of 1952 was different from the one I had left. William Langer had gone back to Harvard at the end of 1951. Under Sherman Kent the operation was even less directed and more collegial. Sherman seemed almost to avoid telling anyone what to do. He spouted out suggestions like a fountain but always with an accompanying argument that invited rebuttal. Sherman's manner—his exaggerated vehemence, the rollicking obscenity, the tugging at his suspenders, and jerking at his tie—seemed to invite a playful response, and we were sometimes surprised to find him deadly serious about a position he had stated comically. He was not so much a leader as a gadfly and a preceptor. His concepts of right and wrong in intelligence estimating were rigorous: no policy direction, no shading evidence or slanting analysis to reach a desired conclusion, no slipshod writing or shortcuts. On these matters he would become very heated, but most of the time he sported and flashed around the discussion like a deerfly. It would be difficult to describe how Sherman Kent ran ONE. It somehow seemed to run itself with

Sherman in the middle of the pack. In fact, I never did quite understand how he did it. We felt it was his office; we respected his concept of the office and its goals; but it was different from our reverential regard for William Langer.

Another important change was the emergence of a new force in the person of Abbott Smith. "Force" at first blush seems too dynamic a word to describe the modest, self-effacing Abbott, a down-East Yankee from Maine whose grandfather had been president of Colby College. Abbott was a distinguished historian with two highly regarded books to his credit and a fine musician, graduate of the Eastman School and accompanist on a year's concert tour with an opera singer. But despite his laconic, tweedy demeanor, Abbott was clearly becoming the dominant substantive voice in CIA estimates, not only through the power of his pragmatic mind but also by the example of his prose style. He wrote a marvelously lucid prose, almost entirely unadorned, direct as speech, quickened occasionally with a mild colloquialism. Rather like the spring-water-clear prose of *New Yorker* essayist E. B. White, but without the quirky twinkle. It is only a slight exaggeration to say that Abbott Smith single-handedly created the style of CIA estimates in the fifties and sixties.

It was Abbott who introduced into our lexicon such freedoms as the use of "say" to introduce an example, as in: "the exact number of nuclear warheads is uncertain but sizeable—say, one thousand." To some of our academicians this seemed racy, but to the staff it struck just the right note consistent with our inconclusive evidence. When discussions became knotted and snarled over language, we often sent for Abbott. He came modestly into the room, listened for a while, and then wrote a paragraph that sliced through the difficulties. Sometimes one of the contestants would complain that the best part of his argument had been left out. "But you don't need that," Abbott would explain. "You don't have to spell that out for people of the level we write for." This leaving things out, or "agreement through exclusion," as I began to think of it, removed a lot of clutter and at its best served to focus attention sharply on the central point, not the background. But it also had shortcomings as it tended toward bloodless abstraction, a tendency that seemed to increase with the passing years until I felt justified in taunting Sherman Kent one day in 1970 with the quip, "There hasn't been a fact in a national intelligence estimate in five years!"

In this changed environment in ONE, my immediate task was to assume direction of the Far East staff. I sat down at my new desk in South Building one day in August 1952 and undertook an estimate on Thailand. Before me were sections already prepared by Far East staff members, James Graham and Harold Ford. My job was to knit together a piece that would simplify the Byzantine complexities of politics as practiced by the Thai military oligarchy and to set forth some home truths about Thai attitudes toward us and the Chinese communists. I had never seen Thailand, had never to my knowledge met a Thai, but I had in my hands all the intelligence the United States possessed on Thailand, and I did not doubt that something useful would emerge.

After Thailand, we turned to the Philippines and the Huk rebellion. And after that to Burma and General Ne Win's problems with communist terrorists in the northeast provinces, then to Indonesia and the question of when the first postindependence elections would be held, on to South Korea and the life expectancy of Syngman Rhee, to Malaya and the Chinese terrorist campaign, to China and the enigma of communist control. During the ensuing year a steady rhythm of work developed, with the slow, wandering beginning of each new estimate and the rising tempo of activity, including rush work at night to keep the schedule, culminated by the meeting of the U.S. Intelligence Board, followed by the brief satisfaction of having produced another national intelligence estimate.

Throughout the year the feeling grew in me that I needed to see the Far East myself. Jim Graham had served in Japan after the war; Hal Ford had worked in Thailand; Chet Cooper, my predecessor on the staff, had been with OSS in China. I was at a severe disadvantage. My firsthand knowledge of the lands bordering the Pacific Ocean did not extend beyond Catalina Island. I took soundings as to the feasibility of arranging a trip for myself and learned that it would be far easier if I were to accompany a board member. Fortunately, we had a new board member, Lieutenant General Harold Bull, my commandant of the National War College, who had retired from the Army upon completing his tenure at NWC in 1952 and had accepted Bedell Smith's invitation to join our board. General Bull, I found, would be happy to travel and also happy to turn the details of itinerary over to me. By September 1953 we had everything arranged, and we took off for San Francisco on a sparkling October morning.

It is difficult for me now to recapture the romance and excitement of that first trip to the Far East. In fact, it would be impossible if it were not for the notes I took—almost rapturous in tone—of my first impressions. Getting there was itself quite a different, and more adventurous, experience before the age of jet aircraft. From San Francisco to Hawaii was over eight hours by Boeing Stratocruiser, a throbbing, heavy-bodied aircraft with a tiny cocktail lounge seemingly suspended by a tightly turning circular staircase from the belly of the plane. From Hawaii to Wake Island was eight hours of night flight over the black ocean, reaching for a tiny coral speck that we found at dawn. And from there to Tokyo was another eight hours, with the last hour a thrashing, tossing ride up Tokyo Bay.

We spent ten days in Japan, much of it on the move outside Tokyo. It was a very thorough, hard-working orientation visit with innumerable conversations and inspection tours with Japanese university officials, industrial leaders, farmers and agricultural specialists, and U.S. military chiefs. I found Japan a delight, from the moment I woke up the first morning at the U.S. Army's Hotel Sanno, in midtown Tokyo, and heard the clop-clop of clogs on the feet of passing Japanese. Here it was, a mere eight years after Hiroshima and the humiliation of signing a peace treaty on an American battleship in Tokyo Bay, and the Japanese were already on their way to new heights of prosperity. Tokyo and the surrounding area did not look as devastated as London and Frankfurt did when I saw them a year or two later. Everywhere we saw hard-working Japanese.

At night, at eleven o'clock, the tiny one-room shops near the Sanno Hotel blazed with light and resounded with the banging of hammers on metal shapers as workers repaired the ubiquitous three-wheeled motorcycle trucks. On a main street in Osaka I saw a laborer with a makeshift harness running from his shoulder to a cart loaded with a sixteen-foot steel I-beam, a ten-foot length of large pipe, and several sheets of metal. He was dragging this load up a slight incline. Incredible straining veins stood out on his neck, leg muscles ridged, and deep groans came from his heaving chest. It was a vivid depiction of Japanese determination and capacity for hard work.

Perhaps the strongest impression I received during our visit to Japan was the self-sufficiency of the Japanese farmer. Guided by Wolf Ladejinsky, the embassy agricultural attaché, we inspected an agricultural cooperative in the village of Angyo in Chiba Prefecture. Five hundred families lived on a little over 1,000 acres, averaging out to 2.5 acres or less per family of five to seven people.

The farm we visited totaled 2.5 acres on which was grown enough rice to feed the family and provide a cash crop, vegetables, and a small nursery of ten to a dozen persimmon trees and several other fruits. Like the other tiny farms it was electrified, a single light bulb hanging in the workshed and in the house and a power plug for driving a portable electric motor. With the motor and a set of belts the farmer drove his rice-processing machines—a sorter, thresher, miller, and even a small grinder. The farmer's wife and children planted the rice by hand, painstakingly separating the tiny plants in flats and transplanting them into tight rows in the ground. A self-sufficient agricultural unit.

South Korea in 1953 was a torn, battered country trying to find itself behind the uncertain security of a cease-fire and the armistice negotiations at Panmunjon. It was U.S. Army turf, and Korea was sprinkled with officers who had served under General

79

Bull. He was keenly looking forward to circulating among them. As a matter of fact, I watched my mild, soft-voiced traveling companion transform himself into a stern lieutenant general shortly after we landed at Kimpo air base. The officer assigned to shepherd us presented General Bull with a mimeographed schedule of our three-day visit. In true Army style it had us breakfasting at "0645 hours, enplaning by L-20 aircraft at 0700 hours," and moving from one command post to another at ten-minute intervals. General Bull looked at the mimeographed sheet briefly and handed it back to the lieutenant colonel. "That's ridiculous," he barked. "I'm not going to have that kind of a schedule. Take out two-thirds of that stuff and give me a program that will give us a chance to learn something."

It was also at this point in the journey that General Bull suggested to me that I use the title "doctor" in presenting myself to our hosts. As a working academic I had been schooled not to parade my doctorate. At Cornell and Williams the instructors, the bottom rank of the academic ladder, all were Ph.D.'s but were called "mister." The rest of the faculty, from assistant professor on up, were called "professor." "Doctor" was sometimes used by students as a term of special respect for a senior professor or department head, but otherwise the title was never used. This may have been inverse snobbery in the Ivy League, but it was the tradition I had learned. The difficulty in the strictly hierarchical society of the military, as General Bull pointed out, was that "Mister Smith" gave our hosts no handle with which to take hold of me. Was I General Bull's masseur or his valet or was I a peer who needed to be included in the local commanding general's guest list for dinner? Should I be whisked off to the enlisted men's quarters or ensconced in VIP chambers alongside General Bull? Once General Bull raised the point I remembered that I had observed several back-of-the-hand exchanges between him and our hosts in Camp Zama, in Hokkaido, and now in Seoul. So, from that moment on I carefully introduced myself to military officers as "Doctor Smith," and I realized they received as clear a signal as though I had called myself "corporal" or "colonel."

The Watch on Asia

The nervous uncertainty regarding the permanence of the Korean armistice arrangements in the fall of 1953 could be seen in the faces of General Maxwell Taylor's staff as we sat at dinner. The colonels all looked ragged from exhaustion. James Woolnough, my National War College classmate, was grey and hollow-eyed from months of sixteen-hour days. General Taylor, however, was clear-eyed, calm, lean, precise, firm, but gentle in manner. He presided over his dinner table in the commanding general's mess as though it were a military seminar. After launching a new discussion topic with several lucid sentences, he would turn to one of the eight or ten officers applying himself to his dinner. "What is your opinion on that, White?" Colonel White would set down his fork and respond crisply and to the point. The conversation was pleasant and good-humored but extremely structured. After dinner General Taylor invited us to watch an Esther Williams movie and then excused himself to go to his quarters and read. I fell asleep.

The next day we saw the cutting edge of the U.S. military presence, the forward military positions north of Seoul. We took off from the straight stretch of the half-mile track of the Seoul Race Course in an L-20, a high-winged, single-engine liaison plane. With considerable straining and throbbing the little plane churned up clouds of dust from the dirt track and lifted itself over the curving fence and the corrugated iron roofs of the clustered shacks at the end of the track. If I had not been an anxious witness and passenger I would not have thought it possible.

Leaving Seoul the valley leading north was sprawling and shapeless, the bordering mountains bare and raw. The nearby hills were pockmarked with artillery emplacements and pimpled with strange little mounds that turned out to be Korean graves. From the air Seoul lay vast and slovenly with only the nearby mountains to provide form and delineation.

We put down at the strip serving the command post of the Twenty-fifth Division, the most forward position, where General Oakes, commanding general of the Twenty-fifth, provided a helicopter for an inspection of his force dispositions. From the air the terrain looked like a military maneuver and exercise ground. The

U.S. Army by then had had many months to establish itself, and the engineers had almost outdone themselves. Each hillock seemed to have an observation post, and behind every hill was an artillery emplacement. All were serviced by trim little gravel roads and helicopter pads. The tightly curving roads leading up to the command posts were lined with whitewashed stones. Despite the parade-ground appearance, the military situation was real, complete with a visible enemy. After a flight down the southern edge of the Demilitarized Zone we landed at a forward observation post and observed with field glasses a body of Chinese communist soldiers and trucks working on a boat landing on the Imjin River.

My special interest while in Korea was to discuss some of the troubling aspects of the political situation. Shortly before our departure from Washington we had completed a special national intelligence estimate in which we had voiced our concern about the Syngman Rhee regime whose heavy-handed autocratic style was stifling progress toward more democratic and more stable government. We also noted extensive corruption that could greatly reduce the effectiveness of U.S. aid and rehabilitation. The officers in Ambassador Ellis Briggs's embassy were reassuring on these points. Rhee's freedom for dictatorial action had been curtailed, they felt, by a series of measures they had imposed on the aging South Korean president, the "father of his country." On the corruption question they shrugged their shoulders, pointing out that a fairly high level of corruption was endemic in the Far East, and they suggested that steady vigilance was the only feasible option for the United States.

In retrospect it seems surprising that there was not a greater recognition of the enormity of the destabilizing shocks the Koreans had endured. Korea had been a unified country for centuries until its division in 1945 into Chinese and American zones. Now, a scant eight years later and immediately after a devastating three-year war, which had wrought great damage to its capital city and to much of the country, we were asking for high standards of democratic government. It seems now that we almost took it for granted that the millions of Koreans living south of the thirty-eighth parallel would enter joyously into the creation of a *semi*-Korea, a *half* Korea called South Korea and would reject the northern half their ancestors had ruled and freely moved about in. I have no explanation for this blindness except to suggest that in the midst of the Eisenhower era in the 1950s it seemed plausible that in the American Age we could guide the half-countries spawned by World War II—South Korea, South Vietnam, and West Germany—up the rocky slopes and onto the high ground of independent democracy, American style. After the miasma of Watergate and the collapse of the American spirit under the Nixon administration, this world view seems incredibly naive and parochial. Not to mention, wrong.

The most memorable American official I met in Seoul was C. Tyler Wood, head of the aid mission. His kindly, sad-eyed, heavy-wrinkled face reminded me of a basset hound. Over drinks before dinner in his single, medium-sized room in the ramshackle Chosen Hotel, in the heart of the ruined city, he played records constantly on a small, portable high-fi. He listened raptly to a Mendelssohn violin concerto, beaming at each of his guests in turn, a warm-hearted, generous-spirited man, deeply lonely in being away from his family in this Godforsaken land but determined to stick it out with his wholly unpleasant job and somehow make it succeed. The Sisyphus-like nature of the rehabilitation task confronting Ty Wood overwhelmed me as he described it. Not only was each rebuilding project in itself formidable, but each required the most fundamental preparation before it could be begun. Each new effort required him to start back somewhere before the beginning. Take, for example, his reforestation program designed to replace the forests that generations of wood-gathering Korean peasants had depleted. The first step was to obtain, by manufacture or purchase, bicycles. *Bicycles?* Yes, bicycles, so that the police could protect the forest preserves from marauders. So, bicycle factories were needed to be built, and for their construction, building materials were. . . . With this primitive level as the starting point in 1953, the economic well-being South Korea achieved in little more than a decade strikes me as a tremendous American achievement.

Our next stop was Taiwan where Ambassador Karl Rankin seemed to experience little difficulty in restraining his enthusiasm in greeting us. I found Taiwan depressing in 1953, perhaps because I arrived with a solid set of preconceptions. The Office of National Estimates had already begun to point out to the Eisenhower administration the illusory base on which the Chiang Kai-shek government based its claim to legitimacy: the imminent return to the Chinese mainland and the resumption of power. We saw this as a hollow claim, believing the Chinese nationalists had neither the military capability to mount an amphibious invasion and a winning campaign on the mainland nor the political appeal to guarantee the support of the Chinese people. On Taiwan itself the political situation was equally unpromising. Eight million Taiwanese at the end of World War II had been relieved of fifty years of Japanese occupation, an occupation that, though benevolent for the most part, was still exploitive, only to find themselves in 1950 subjected to the dominance of two million mainlanders.

This was not, it ought to be made clear, the subjugation of a native population quite different ethnically and culturally from the invaders. Actually, the resident Taiwanese, except for a few thousand indigenous tribal people of ancient Malay stock, were no more native than the newly arrived mainlanders. The Taiwanese were merely the descendants of earlier Chinese migrations in the eighteenth and nineteenth centuries, mostly from Canton, Hokkien, and Szechuan provinces, and their culture was entirely Chinese. There were differences, though, between the two populations that, though more subtle than ethnic, were pervasive and real. The islanders spoke the dialect of their native provinces (Cantonese, Hokkienese), while the newcomers spoke Mandarin, the dialect of culture and learning; the islanders were southerners and farmers and fishermen while the mainlanders were northerners and bureaucrats, soldiers, and professional men. The frictions were considerable, and the Chiang Kai-shek regime, keenly aware of this resentment as well as the constant threat of subversion by communist infiltrators, maintained a heavy, relentless police repression. Arriving with this knowledge, I did not expect to find Taiwan very appealing.

Nothing I heard in Taiwan altered my jaundiced view. But if my intellectual reactions to Taiwan were negative, my sensual responses were vibrant. It began with the lovely fragrances that wafted through the Grand Hotel from the garden outside. It was an odor of pungent, green leaves and tea blossoms, and I had never known so exotic a smell before nor have I since. Our rooms glowed with the sheen of highly polished, wide-planked teak floors and the reflection of vibrantly Chinese red columns outside our large windows. And then the Chinese women! It was my first glimpse of young Chinese girls in *cheong sams*—lightweight sheaths of half-calf length slit about four inches above the knees and fitted skin tight across the hips. When they rode bicycles or sat in pedicabs they exposed about half their thigh. Their skin, I noted, was a lovely golden tan, about the color most American girls strive to attain in the sun. Why, I asked myself, do we call the Chinese *yellow?* Also, I noted in my journal with a scientific detachment equal to Charles Darwin's, that "there is no available evidence to suggest Chinese girls wear anything under their sheaths."

The physical beauty of Taiwan was stunning. The mountainsides were lush with bamboo groves, firs, casurinas, rush grasses, and ferns, and below lay an opulent valley, knee-deep in rice fields of great number and incredible fertility. Off to the east loomed the dark-blue mountains that plunged steeply into the sea on the eastern side of the island. On the slopes fine misty showers made brilliant rainbows as the droplets floated down through the sunshine. I had never seen such beauty.

Hong Kong lay a similar spell on this first-time visitor to the East. From the time we boarded the Star Ferry until we left four days later I felt almost as though I were running a slight fever. The atmosphere of Hong Kong was so electric, the smells, images, and sounds so sensuous and so totally exotic, that my mind reeled and tumbled: the heaving of the green sea water alongside the ferry as it threaded its way among junks with their slatted sails, under the counters of large freighters swinging slowly at anchor and alongside tiny boats sculled by a single oar, the enchanting smell of cooking Chinese food wafting from the little pushcarts alongside the streets, the boisterously red rickshaws standing in close ranks beside the ferry entrance, the hum and clatter of the bustling city, still audible across the water as we moved out from the dock and across the magical harbor.

In 1953, the lobby of the Peninsula Hotel still looked like a stage setting for a Somerset Maugham play dramatizing the last great days of the British Empire. The substance and power of Empire were gone, consumed by the long war the British fought between 1939 and 1945, but the outer facade remained. The large lobby, filled with people moving about or sitting and talking, was furnished in a heavy, solid style with potted palms everywhere. At teatime a string orchestra played 1920s tunes as decorous background to the chink of teacups and silver spoons.

General Bull and I had enormous rooms with balconies overlooking the harbor. A British cruiser lay off to the left, its boatswain whistle sounding from time to time with a subsequent crackle of the ship's public address system. A great black-and-red freighter moved slowly into a mooring as two tugs hooted and bustled about. All the while the green and white ferries moved ceaselessly back and forth, picking their way around and through the busy traffic. Across the water the lights of Hong Kong glittered and sparkled at the water's edge and soared high up into the blackness of the peak., I fell under an enchantment with Hong Kong from which I've never recovered.

Our business discussions in Hong Kong almost entirely concerned the operations of the China-watching group. Hong Kong became an American watchtower on China shortly after the communists took power in 1949 and closed the doors to diplomatic representation. Through a systematic program of combing through provincial newspapers, debriefing knowledgeable refugees, and gar-

86

nering family gossip among the Hong Kong Chinese community, it was possible to form some general understanding of what was happening inside that vast country, tightly shut against the Western world. In actuality, the China-watchers had few advantages that analysts in Washington did not have. But they did have propinquity to China itself, not an insignificant advantage. From the northern portions of the Hong Kong Leased Territories, one can gaze at nearby mountains that look down on that enormous, teeming land. At the railway bridge in Kowloon, one can watch the daily arrival of the train and a clutch of passengers. In Washington, by contrast, intelligence analysts looked at yellow sheets of paper bearing typed messages. We had extended talks with the China-watchers during which I was able to give them insights into Washington's current preoccupations, and they gave me a set of requests to take back.

The bittersweet contrast between the faded trappings of British imperial rule and the present was again displayed during our day with General Sir William Airey, commander of British forces in Hong Kong. General Airey, a well-starched, mustachioed, pleasant man, met us in the lobby of the Peninsula Hotel and escorted us to his long, black Pullman Humber limousine. We set off for an inspection of the British military defenses for Hong Kong. They consisted of a series of prepared positions high in the hills of the Leased Territories, connected by a set of jeep-type trails, and serviced by a north-south military road. During our inspection we visited a Ghurka camp, and I tried to imagine how long this small detachment of little brown men, fierce fighters though they are, could hold off hordes of Chinese soldiers. It was the "pane of glass" concept indeed, a symbol that existed only to be shattered, and well understood by General Airey so to be.

But this did not cause him to alter in the slightest the demeanor and lifestyle of the commander of a British imperial force. After our inspection trip we lunched at General Airey's residence, Flagstaff House. At this charming, gracious dwelling, built in 1840 on the edge of the Hong Kong business district, lunch was splendid. It began appropriately with a gin and lime, progressed through lobster soup and sherry to rare roast beef and beer, and concluded with cognac. Echoes of the great days of the British Raj reverberated silently in my head.

Bangkok, our next stop, was the first place we visited where the work of the U.S. Embassy was not dominated by military concerns and a military command and its ancillary intelligence organization. In Thailand, intelligence-gathering activities were free from the narrow focus a military command requires, and the officers could cast their nets in any direction to garner information about threats to U.S. interests in Southeast Asia. It was here I met firsthand an endemic problem for intelligence work overseas: lack of precise and accurate guidance. The focus in Thailand was entirely on local concerns instead of the broader strategic concerns that engaged us in Washington. I promised I would try to have better guidance provided after I returned to headquarters.

Our visit to Thailand was otherwise memorable only for a remarkable story told us by the American consul in Chieng Mai, a lovely town we hoped would give us some insight and under-standing of upcountry Thailand. We had left Bangkok on the evening train, sharing a compartment in a British sleeper coach built in Sheffield in 1921, the dark wood paneling creaking evocatively with the movement of the car. All night long we climbed long hills and crossed long, spindly trestles over gorges cut deep in the jungle, and arrived in Chieng Mai in early afternoon, four hundred miles and twenty hours from Bangkok. The American consul, a young, open-faced, red-haired man, met us and took us to his residence for a drink and conversation. I was curious about the duties of an American consul in a remote post like Chieng Mai and asked what work there was to do. The consul was loaded for this question and proceeded to lecture me severely for the next forty minutes, much to General Bull's delight.

It seemed that within a few days after their arrival the consul's wife, then five months' pregnant, contracted polio. She elected not to return to the United States, and the American doctors at the Seventh-day Adventist Hospital in Chieng Mai endorsed this, provided she could have daily therapy in a large bathtub. It developed there was not a bathtub to be found in Chieng Mai because Thai people bathe with hand-held basins scooped into large cisterns. Finally, an American-made tub was located in Bangkok and freighted north.

While the consul was struggling with this problem and its many ramifications, his only assistant in the two-man post became ill and died overnight. His widow insisted that her husband's body be shipped back to the United States for burial. Then the consul discovered that there was no Western-style undertaker in Chieng Mai and no facilities for embalming the body. He sought the assistance of the American doctors at the Seventh-day Adventist Hospital, one of whom produced a textbook, with appropriate directions, and together the consul and the doctor did the embalming. Then came the problem of the coffin, an article not commercially available. The consul proceeded to design and supervise the construction of a suitable coffin by a Thai cabinetmaker. The widow was too grief-stricken to make her own travel arrangements or those of the deceased so our man had this final chore to accomplish. All these terrible events occurred during the first two weeks of his stay in Chieng Mai. "And that," he said in conclusion, "are the duties of an American consul in Chieng Mai." General Bull never let me forget the horrendous tale my question had produced.

Singapore, our next stop, proved to be both a surprise and a professional bonanza for me. First, the surprise. Conditioned by grade-B movies and Joseph Conrad's novels, I had envisioned Singapore as a murky, slatternly place, peopled by sinister Chinese who lived in corrugated-roof shacks looking over a harbor crowded with rusty coastal freighters and decrepit junks. The contrast, the reality, could not have been greater. The harbor, for example, as seen from the U.S. naval attaché's launch, was very large and orderly. Most ships loaded at long, modern docks. Small coasters anchored out in the harbor and lightered their cargo ashore, but the whole operation looked systematic and—in a word—unromantic.

Even the legendary Raffles Hotel turned out to be a pleasant stone structure, not bamboo and attap fronds, and the air conditioning at the Elizabethan Grill was so aggressive it froze us stiff at lunch. Not that the outside temperature was terribly hot. Singapore is a scant seventy miles north of the Equator, but a steady sea breeze over the island keeps the thermometer mostly below ninety, about eighty-five or so. At dinner that night we sat at white-clothed tables on the lawn and marveled at the absence of insects circling the kerosene torches. The other guests expanded at length about the delightful living in Singapore, "the finest residential city in the Far East." I made a mental note.

The professional bonanza came in the realization of Singapore's significance in the mid-1950s as a strategic center in Southeast Asia. Singapore was far more than an entrepot. For the British it was both a bastion of commercial-financial interests and a regional defense center. In 1953, Singapore was still a Crown colony, and Malaya and North Borneo were British possessions. For the Americans, Singapore had mostly commercial values, but its importance in long-term strategic terms was evident in Washington. For both, it was a unique window on the swirling post-World War II scene of Southeast Asia where every country from Burma to Indonesia was struggling to reach a new accommodation with changed realities. It seemed to me that an observer with a broad substantive background, situated in Singapore, could provide perspectives and insights of value. Through his immersion in the local scene and his normal contacts with merchants, shipping men, military officers, and diplomats he could gain an understanding of the interplay of economic, political, and strategic forces as seen from *within* the region, not from distant and paperbound Washington. I made another mental note.

The second professional bonus came during our visit to the headquarters of General William Templer in Kuala Lumpur. An important question for Washington in 1953 was how well the British were doing in quelling the guerrilla insurgency in Malaya. Our judgment in CIA was that the British were making very slow progress and had months, possibly years, of dangerous fighting before they could end the Emergency, as the British called it. Moreover, we feared that the ongoing terrorist movement could spread both north and south and infect Thailand and Singapore.

What I discovered, as I sat in the spartan briefing room of General Templer's headquarters, was that the British had almost put out the fire. Arrayed on a wooden map of Malaya were the names of the known communist terrorists, "CTs" in 1953 terms, each name hung on a little hook marking the center of his radius of activity. There were only forty or fifty. The British knew them all by name, had identified their families and their circle of acquaintances, and knew their skills and weaknesses. And this, except for an occasional fisherman or farmer who was co-opted and forced to help, was the entire remaining strength of the communist insurgency in Malaya in 1953.

As the American colonel who accompanied us to the briefing remarked, the insurgency had been whittled down to such a level that combatting it was comparable to trying to arrest all the burglars in Toledo or Kansas City. This was surprising news indeed, and I found strong resistance to accepting it as unvarnished truth when I got back to Washington. Not only had it never been reported by cable (cause for doubt in itself among paperbound analysts), but there was also a pervading reluctance to believe that communists anywhere ever faltered and fell short of their objectives. Such a suggestion in 1953 was suspected of being soft-headed.

General Templer's briefing set forth in crisp detail how this feat was being accomplished. There were three key tactical elements the British had hand-tailored for the situation in Malaya: first, food denial—farmers, rubber tappers, and their families were moved inside stockades where they could be protected from marauders. Cans of food purchased at a store were opened immediately by the storekeeper so that they had to be consumed within hours before they spoiled in the jungle heat. Second, precise intelligence obtained by work so exhaustingly thorough that a single individual could be located in the midst of an almost impenetrable jungle.

Third, inhuman patience—often eight or nine weeks passed before the quarry moved after a ring had been set.

Later, in the 1960s and 1970s, Americans often wondered why the British success in Malaya could not be emulated in Vietnam. The stock answer was that the basic circumstances were different: in Malaya the terrorists were an ethnic minority (Chinese) who were readily distinguishable from the majority Malays, but in Vietnam the terrorists were dissident members of the majority Vietnamese. This is certainly true and a key difference, but it is also true that the rebellion had political and social roots. Consequently the British fashioned a response that coordinated municipal controls and local police action with army operations, creating a net that closed around the terrorists from every side. In Vietnam, the Americans followed the French lead and responded almost solely in military terms—conventional military terms, at that—until late in the game, by which time the movement had acquired substantial momentum. I am proud to say that CIA analysts and estimators recognized this fundamental truth about the social and political roots of the struggle in Vietnam from the beginning and held this view undeviatingly throughout the period of American involvement.

I must not leave Singapore without mentioning a memorable Saturday afternoon at the Singapore Racing Club where I observed a slice of Singapore society, a postwar society in transition. In our box were a number of Chinese and American women, all mixing easily and enjoying each other's company, symbolic in a way of the post-war shift in the social hierarchy of Singapore. Off to our left was a group of frumpy British women, the pre-war elites, wives of local businessmen, clustered by themselves and betting seriously but moderately on their favorite horses. The Chinese women were gay and sophisticated and included one sensationally beautiful young woman, fortunately sitting beside me, who was slim as a willow and whose *cheong sam* was fitted to the smallest ripple of her golden skin. This was Christine Lok, wife of Lok Wan Tho, a Singapore film magnate and world-class photographer of wild birds. I have never seen a more lovely creature.

Our next stop was Djakarta, and there awaited me another important truth, as important as my discovery regarding the Emergency in Malaya, but one I failed to recognize at the time and did not fully hoist aboard for a number of years. This had to do with the prospects and future courses of President Sukarno, who had wrested independence from Dutch colonial rule immediately after World War II. Back in Washington, CIA estimators viewed with gentle approving eye Sukarno's efforts to consolidate his revolution against three centuries of Dutch rule. We excused his theatrical flair and self-aggrandizing posturing as essential in establishing leadership over that wide-flung archipelago. He was the George Washington of Indonesia.

From this perspective I listened with approval to the U.S. Embassy political officers who stressed the tremendous obstacles Sukarno had to overcome to unify his country and establish a constitutional democracy. By contrast, the views of another officer, an attaché, were alarmist. He saw Sukarno first and foremost as a self-appointed dictator who would stop at nothing to maintain his position. He foresaw an inevitable slide to the left as Sukarno, striving to avoid an electoral defeat, would abandon the moderates looking for democratic rule and seek the support of the communist-led left. I should have listened attentively to him because history has proved him brilliantly right.

It might be argued, of course, that Sukarno's swerve to the left was not inevitable, that subsequent events may have pushed him in a direction counter to his instincts and intentions. But in retrospect, the "balanced" view ignored plainly visible dynamics in Sukarno's character and placed too much trust in his presumed statesmanlike qualities. Possibly we also minimized the staggering problems involved in establishing a freely democratic regime in a newly independent country with the geographic and ethnic obstacles Indonesia faced. We may have been, like most Americans, who are immersed from time of birth in the hard-won privileges, attitudes, and procedures of a democratic society, naive about the ease with which subjugated, colonial people can adopt democratic forms and processes. More than a mere desire to be "free" is required. The American frontier ethos and pioneer mythology tend to blind us to the strong disciplinary and personal restraint elements inherent in our system. Democratic government must be earned and achieved, not merely aspired to.

The physical aspects of central Djakarta were miserable. It was a sloppy, unkempt city with scum-covered ditches beside the main roads. But the suburbs were better, with quiet, leafy streets, and stuccoed houses enclosed by low garden walls. While I breakfasted with my host, a young embassy officer, the bright morning air rang with the cries of passing street vendors and hawkers, a steady succession of calls, hoots, and shouts. Flowers, vegetables, balloons, live birds, fish—everything the local market offered—went by on the shoulders of the street criers.

Our host and program-manager at our next stop, Saigon, was Rob McClintock, my National War College classmate and sailing companion. McClintock was deputy chief of mission under Ambassador Donald Heath. Through his thoughtful planning and a bit of serendipity General Bull and I witnessed the rising of the curtain on one of the most dramatic and pivotal events in history, one that directly led to the French withdrawal from Vietnam and the American assumption of the burden there.

Our first appointment in Saigon was with General Navarre, commander of French forces in Vietnam. Eyes sparkling in his narrow, aristocratic face, General Navarre described to us a newly launched operation that promised great success. It was taking place at a remote town in North Vietnam known as Dien Bien Phu. The locale was perfect from the French point of view, he told us. For weeks he had been waiting for the Viet Minh to walk into this trap. Intelligence had told Navarre that Viet Minh Division 316 was headed for Dien Bien Phu, so he responded quickly and got there first. The region was a rich rice-producing center, he explained, a "breadbasket," the only place in that particular area that could feed a division. By denying it to the Viet Minh, he had spelled their doom. *"Le pauvre Viet Minh 316!"* he said in his quick, precise French with a droll smile. "What will they do now?" He felt they had no choice but to attack the well-prepared, well-entrenched French forces, and they would suffer severe losses and a costly defeat.

General Navarre's enthusiasm for the Dien Bien Phu operation was so great that he insisted that General Bull visit the scene during our forthcoming trip to the north. He commanded an aide to get him General Cogny on the telephone, General Cogny then being the general in command of operations in the north from his headquarters in Hanoi. A brief, rapid-fire conversation with Cogny ensued, and from Navarre's end of it, both McClintock and I got the impression that Cogny was unenthusiastic about taking American visitors into Dien Bien Phu. "Some temporary difficulty with the airstrip," Navarre explained when he had finished, "but he will receive you and arrange it."

It was only after my return to Washington that I learned from my CIA colleagues that the "temporary difficulty with the airstrip" had been created by the emplacement of Viet Minh artillery in the hills enclosing the plain at Dien Bien Phu. These guns were actually shooting the tails off French aircraft and tearing up the landing strip. Previous to the first bursts on the hapless French, the Viet Minh were believed not to have artillery. No wonder the optimistic French were surprised to the point of shock.

General Bull managed eventually to distract Navarre's soaring enthusiasm by asking him about Viet Minh attack techniques. Here, Navarre was fascinating. Viet Minh attacks consisted of a rapid series of punches, he said, always at night. Before attacking a place, they studied it inside and out until they knew every feature of its construction and the daily routines. Then they withdrew and constructed a model against which they rehearsed the attack again and again, fifteen times or more. Then, if anything were to go wrong during the actual attack they would stop the operation at once and withdraw. They mounted only set pieces, Navarre said.

Next morning McClintock had arranged that we would visit the Emperor Bao Dai, the French puppet ruler of Vietnam. We flew up to Ban Me Thuot in the plush Embassy DC-3, complete with sofa and carpeting. At the last minute, former Ambassador William Bullitt joined the party, somewhat to the irritation of Ambassador Heath and McClintock, who felt that Bullitt's presence in Vietnam owed more to private business interests than to U.S. national policy. At Ban Me Thuot we were met by Bao Dai's *chef de cabinet* who informed us that the emperor was not well but that he would receive us at his hunting lodge by a lake some fifty kilometers distant.

We set out in two cars through a driving rain on an incredible journey through the jungle. The road was no more than a mud track, lined on either side with deep water ditches, and we slithered and slid all over it as our young Vietnamese driver drove at breakneck speed. Every few hundred yards we crossed a narrow bridge on two slippery planks. Several times, during a particularly wide slither or a skid on a bridge I resigned myself to the certainty of an accident. I was also pretty certain that we were possibly subject to Viet Minh grenade or machine-gun attack in that wild terrain. About halfway there we came to a wide stream serviced by a small ferry. The two cars were jammed on with their bumpers hanging out over the water, and three reddish brown little men in loin cloths—more loin than cloth—began pushing us across the current with long poles. The rain slanted down hard, and as it struck their bare backs, it made dark wet streaks.

The Emperor Bao Dai greeted us splendidly, dressed in a grey sport coat, blue sport shirt, grey slacks, and very fancy black-and-white sport shoes. A moon-faced man of 35 or 40, he did not look unwell as he lambasted French neglect, pursing his lips and making rapid little shakes of his head like an indignant maiden aunt. He was aided and encouraged in his diatribe against the French by Ambassador Bullitt who spoke a very rapid, authentically accented French (but grammatically very bad, Rob McClintock later told me). This dismayed Donald Heath who spoke a French somewhat more like mine, halting and bearing the accent of a midwestern high school. Heath, the accredited and responsible ambassador, tried repeatedly and with little success to halt Bao Dai's and Bullitt's gallop over the wreckage of French intentions and to introduce some moderation into the discourse, beginning every sentence with, *"Mais . . ."* Pursing his liver-colored lips and shaking his head, Bao Dai rushed on, urged and encouraged by Bullitt's voluble if ungrammatical French.

What he needed, the emperor in sports shoes said, was full political independence in some kind of association with the French. But *not* a French Union. Perhaps a Union of Free States. He waxed bitter about French colonial attitudes toward him and "his people."

After an hour's worth of imperial audience we loaded back into the cars and slithered back to Ban Me Thuot. We took off from the soggy grass runway in the driving rain and landed miraculously intact in Saigon. We spent the next day in Saigon being briefed by the U.S. military aid mission who groused ferociously about the French utilization of military equipment (only one crew per aircraft as compared to the U.S. 2.7 average; thirty hours of airtime per month contrasted with the USAF's eighty to ninety).

It was Thanksgiving Day, 1953, when we took off at dawn for Haiphong. There we transferred to a French Air Force DC-3, loaded to the wing struts with baggage and people. Somehow the old plane thrashed itself into the air, and we made the short flight to Hanoi, making a sporting landing there, remarkable in that the pilot did not cut the throttles until we were on the runway, the first time I had ever landed at the same speed I took off.

Our host in Hanoi was the U.S. consul general, Paul Sturm, who greeted us with conspicuous reserve. A very small man and customarily prickly, Sturm was further irritated by our coming in on him on Thanksgiving Day. He was endeavoring to put on an American-style Thanksgiving dinner for his small staff, complete with roast turkey and mince pie. These American culinary specialties were alien, exotic concoctions to the Vietnamese cook, so the consul general was forced to add cooking to his other duties, and this did not gentle his disposition. He took time off from the kitchen to accompany us for an interview with General Cogny.

Once again we heard about the great opportunities Dien Bien Phu offered the French, but General Cogny demurred at the prospect of giving us a chance to see for ourselves. There had been a small difficulty in clearing the airstrip at Dien Bien Phu, Cogny observed, so he had made arrangements for us to go down to Sept Pagodes in the Red River Delta where we could observe a sweep operation in progress. He referred to a large wall map behind him to point out its location. What immediately struck me was that the map was almost entirely covered with red splotches denoting Viet Minh dominance. The clear areas consisted mostly of the Hanoi-Haiphong axis, vital to the French for the rail transfer of seaborne supplies from Haiphong harbor, and a "good" area west and somewhat south of Hanoi. But this evidence did not visibly dismay General Cogny who was six-feet four-inches tall, spoke with rapid ebullience, and gave off an aura of hard-packed power. Where General Navarre had seemed lean, laconic, and deadly, Cogny was robust and hearty.

Paul Sturm's Thanksgiving dinner for his little band and the two visiting Americans in the beleagured outpost of Hanoi in 1953 was a great success. The turkey was roasted to perfection, and although the mince pie was a little strange, it was recognizably mince pie. General Bull performed the role of "papa" and carved the turkey in masterful fashion. In the spirit of festivity created by this occasion of a group of Americans observing a national holiday in an excessively foreign land, Paul Sturm mellowed and thawed notably. Later, as I lay in bed before falling asleep, I could hear the steady firing of guns in the night.

Next morning we set out to observe the French Union army in the field. At Bac Mai airport we were met by French officers and led to a battered single-engine aircraft. General Bull and I huddled in tandem behind the pilot who had a carbine at his side. After takeoff I noted that the pilot circled over Bac Mai until we reached four thousand or five thousand feet and then flew strictly over the Hanoi-Haiphong highway where he could be fairly certain he would not receive Viet Minh ground fire.

At Sept Pagodes we landed on a tiny dirt strip. We boarded a jeep and took our place in a small convoy—armored car front and rear followed by a squad of soldiers in a truck—and we shot off on the roughest goddammed ride I ever had. The driver flipped back and forth on the road avoiding deep pockmarks from mines and shells and drove as fast as the surface would permit. All along the route sentinels and patrols manned the ridges. As we arrived at the camp inside the barbed-wire perimeter I noted a group of twelve 105-mm guns, but I was quite unprepared as three of them fired almost simultaneously just as I was disembarking from the jeep. I was almost on my knees before I recovered control.

The commander of the mobile brigade, Colonel Roumiantzoff, gave us a briefing in the command tent. His unit had been undertaking a sweep through a guerrilla-infested area when it ran into a Viet Minh regular battalion, apparently being rested. The unit had no knowledge that the VM battalion was there, and by the time they got themselves sorted out it was night and the VM pulled out. They had lost eight dead and fifty-two wounded in the opening encounter. As we arrived, they were mopping up against VM regionals and irregulars, the guns firing on demand from forward observers. All around the camp, radio and wireless receivers squawked and beeped, and beside every tent and armored vehicle inside the barbed-wire perimeter was a foxhole. The unit had come under mortar fire the previous night and expected to do so again that night.

Against this backdrop of hair-trigger readiness, it was astonishing that two orderlies then cleared the table of battle maps and covered it with a snowy white tablecloth. Places were set with silver and cloth napkins while we were having the first of several aperitifs. Then followed a pleasant, prolonged lunch of several courses, wine by the tumbler-full, concluded with brandy and cigars.

The esprit and camaraderie of the group was impressive. One of the officers, the commander of the Foreign Legion battalion, who sat at the table pale, nervous, and distracted, had nearly broken down under fire the night before and had been relieved. Colonel Roumiantzoff, the brigade commander, teased him gently from time to time in a fatherly fashion. The others were relaxed and buoyant.

While we were eating, word came in that a tank destroyer had hit a mine, and some men were injured. The doctor got up from the table and went out by jeep. He returned minutes later saying that the damage was not serious, largely shock and concussion. One of the pieces of information I had brought with me to Vietnam was that the Red River Delta had few roads and what few there were had been systematically destroyed by the Viet Minh. This was much more forcefully borne out when the French surgeon told me, after his return, that he had been unable to evacuate the wounded from last night's action. He and a group of bearers were going into the battle area after dark, using the dikes on the rice paddies as pathways, to carry the wounded out on their backs. While we sat over a leisurely lunch, the wounded had been lying out there unattended.

It was nearly three o'clock when we finished our brandies, and Colonel Roumiantzoff insisted we leave in order to be well on our way back to Hanoi before darkness fell and action resumed. Back we scurried, the jouncing jeep ride and the tiny airplane flight no less stimulating because they were in reverse order from our trip down. When we arrived unharmed at the consulate residence and I could shift my attention from survival to reflection, I realized that I had witnessed a memorable demonstration of French military operations in Vietnam. Unforgettable.

After Vietnam, the only remaining country to visit on my Far Eastern "beat" was Burma where our stay was brief and distinctly not memorable. Rangoon in 1953 was a country in postcolonial decay, the streets of the capital city pocked with deep potholes and populated by packs of mangy dogs. In succeeding years, as I watched from my vantage point in CIA while Burma floundered and slipped from one ineptitude to another, I came to feel that among the exotic cultures of Southeast Asia Burma is by far the least accessible for understanding by the Western mind. It is hermetic and inward-directed, shrouded in the mists of Buddhism and animistic superstition, to an almost incomprehensible degree.

The Burmese visit completed my official business as chief of the Far East staff of ONE, but having progressed more than halfway around the world it was sensible to continue westward. General Bull and I, for a mix of reasons, chose New Delhi, Karachi, Cairo, Rome, and Madrid to complete the itinerary.

Several high points of that journey still glow in my memory. The first concerns those few occasions when General Bull and I drank and dined alone. One night in particular we were left to ourselves in the Grande Hotel in Siem Reap, not far from the glooming mysteries of Angkor Wat. After a round or two of Scotch my distinguished companion began to reminisce. Several of the stories I recall provide insightful little footnotes to history. Once in the early 1930s Omar Bradley came striding into a Saturday night party at an Army base somewhere in Texas with some news for his fellow officers, many of whom were to become top generals in World War II. Addressing young captains with names like Eisenhower, Gruenther, Terry Lee, and Bull, Bradley said, "I've been doing some arithmetic today on serial numbers and promotion rates, and I want to tell you that not a man in this room is ever going to rise above the rank of lieutenant colonel."

Aside from a wrong assumption that peacetime promotion rates would prevail during their careers, Bradley's arithmetic had not included another significant factor: the wisdom and judgment of General George C. Marshall. Bull told me that Marshall had been an instructor in tactics at Fort Leavenworth for many years and had observed successive classes of rising Army officers passing through. He had sighted the really good ones and had made notes. In 1939 he visited Culver Military Academy in Indiana where General Bull was commandant at the time. Over dinner he said, "Bull, we all know there is a war coming, and we are going to have to get ready to fight it. I have made a list of the one hundred best officers in the U.S. Army. If I can get that group of men pulled together we will have the best army the world has ever seen." He did, and it may well have been.

About the character of the men who led the U.S. Army in World War II, Bull was sometimes openly enthusiastic and sometimes ambivalent. Concerning Omar Bradley he was always enthusiastic. "Brad was the best of us in everything, the smartest, best horseman, best shot. When he and I went quail shooting, Brad would let me shoot first, and then after I had missed my bird he would knock his down and then swing and get mine."

He was also warm in his feelings toward General Bedell Smith who was remembered by most officers as the tough son of a bitch who was Eisenhower's chief of staff and hatchet man. "Beedle was a fine man, strong. At the signing of the cease-fire agreement with the Germans in 1945, Beedle and I went into the men's room, and I held his head while he vomited into the toilet bowl. Nothing came out but green bile. He washed his face and went in and presided over the signing ceremony."

About Eisenhower he was reticent. To my questions about what Ike was really like, Bull would respond laughingly that Ike had given him some monumental chewing-outs. Questions related to Kay Summersby, Eisenhower's jeep driver and reputed girlfriend, drew a blank. Discreet suggestions that Mamie Eisenhower might have had a little problem with alcohol—often rumored at that time—caused abrupt irritation. "I never saw any sign of that, *doctor*." (This was as close as General Bull permitted himself to approach sarcasm.) But although there was never a derogatory word about Eisenhower, there was also no sign of affection or anything other than the respect an officer owes his superior officer. Toward George C. Marshall he was reverential.

At the Yalta Conference, General Bull told me, one of his own personal characteristics was given official recognition—his bent for exuberant snoring. "I've always been a loud snorer," he said. "You must have noticed it." Indeed I had and had been trying at every opportunity to get us quartered in separate bedrooms. I had been sufficiently successful up to that point to keep my health intact. But so great was my respect and affection for General Bull that I pretended not to notice and made no complaint. At the Yalta Conference, however, Bull's long-established reputation throughout the Army was recognized when the officer in charge of billeting paired him with the Army's *second* loudest snorer. Bull said people two buildings away could hear the roar when the duet reached top crescendo.

Another shining memory of that trip records my first impressions of India. The visual impact of Delhi and the surrounding countryside was stunning. The astonishing streets jammed with trucks, sagging buses, bicycles, bullock carts, camels, and wandering cows; the overwhelming massiveness and breadth of ancient structures like the Red Fort, the Purana Qila, and Humuyn's Tomb. The countryside pulsed with glowing images: piles of ruins and the crumbling foundations of ancient cities, monkeys chattering in the trees over the roadway and perched on fences at the roadside, flights of green, orange-flecked parrots screeching as they flew over, bony grey cattle feeding dully on scrub bushes, a flock of peacocks sitting on a high wall, farmers threshing grain by driving bullocks round and round over a circular pile on the ground, oxen drawing goatskins of water from a well, pulling the well rope while walking down a sloping ramp, a blindfolded camel circling slowly about a Persian water wheel with its crude, wooden gears. As we drove back into Delhi one afternoon, the long rays of the setting December sun slanted through the dry air and gilded the dust and struck the old towers and crumbling ruins on the vast plain with a searching and enhancing luminosity. India is a photographer's paradise. I thought how much I would like to have a year or more for taking pictures by that extraordinary light. Like my tentative thoughts about Singapore, it was to have an eventual fulfillment, years later.

My first encounter with Richard Nixon occurred on the final stage of this trip. General Bull and I had changed our schedule several times to avoid overlapping with the vice-presidential entourage whose arrival caused embassy staffs and facilities to overload their circuits. But by this time our options were exhausted, and General Bull felt that one night in Karachi would not be an intrusion. All along our way we had heard glowing accounts from embassy officers about the Nixon visit. They were to a man deeply impressed with the vice president's informed understanding of the problems of their country, his receptivity to their views, and his close attention to their briefings. Accustomed to the constant streams of junketing congressmen who thought mostly of getting their hands on local counterpart funds with which to do some luxury shopping, they greatly appreciated dealing with a top official who was serious, informed, and thoughtful.

Vice President Nixon greeted General Bull and me warmly. "I heard you were traveling in the area," he said in that curiously hollow voice, sounding almost as though it came from an echo chamber lined with gauze, "and I hoped you would join us." General Bull responded with his usual modest grace and demurred when the vice president urged him to attend that evening's state dinner with him. "We're just a couple of observers," he said, "looking around."

I had dinner that night with several members of the Nixon staff, notably Rose Mary Woods and Christian Herter, Jr. I was curious as to how the Nixon staff viewed their chief and the arduous trip. They admitted they were tired, having endured two months of moving from country to country with an unending succession of receptions, state dinners, and protocol formalities. "But," I said to Rose Mary Woods, "you must be able to rest between stops on your very comfortable airplane." "Oh, no," she said, "that's when we do most of our work." She went on to describe how the vice president dictated notes about his last visit, studied briefing books for his next, and consulted with an embassy officer from the next post who had flown to meet them and accompany them to his home base. The Nixon staffers keenly admired Patricia Nixon, whose skills as a traveler were considerable. Her formal gowns were kept on hangers in the airplane, never folded in a suitcase; on the flight between stops she got out an ironing board and pressed them afresh. She also washed and ironed the vice president's shirts en route. But more than anything, they appreciated Mrs. Nixon's unfailing graciousness and thoughtfulness.

I must add here a footnote regarding Vice President Nixon's trip and its contribution to his understanding of Far Eastern affairs. My admiration for his earnest efforts to learn about the problems of the area came to an abrupt halt one day back in Washington. I was invited to attend a meeting of Richard Nixon with top State Department officials and congressional leaders. Nixon gave a one-dimensional, anticommunist talk that sounded precisely like what he had been saying for years. It was as though he had learned nothing about the intricacies and subtleties of Far Eastern affairs in two months of traveling but had seen it all through the polarized lens of the communist menace. The chameleon-like transformation from perceptive observer to anticommunist demagogue was total.

A few days after Karachi we were back in Washington. I have recounted some aspects of this journey in such detail because of the sharp contrast between the Far East as it was in the early 1950s and as it is in the 1980s. Just to run through the names of some of the places makes the point:

Japan, then struggling in postwar recovery, and now an industrial and technological giant whose success is menacing to the West;

Vietnam, then a colonial country torn by civil war but still possessed of charming provincial towns and marked by the graces of French colonial culture, and now a battered country ripped by modern warfare and finally entrapped in the vise of communist control, a condition that was virtually unimaginable in 1953;

Thailand, a smiling, fat countenance then, and now a country spoiled by too-rapid modernization and the distortions imposed on the national economy by close proximity to the Vietnam War and a suffocating American presence;

Cambodia, whose loveliness was legendary and entrancing then, but whose cities and people have been ravaged by benighted, ideological zealots; and

Two countries that have changed also in that quarter-century or so but whose changes have generally been for the better: *Malaysia,* a tidy, thriving little country, modernizing at a sensible pace and somehow continuing to manage the communal divisions between Malays and Chinese without severe disruption; and *Singapore,* a spectacularly successful city-state making its way into the modern world with only the territory of a 13-by-8-mile island, a model of cleanliness, efficiency, and intelligent management.

The insights and images I gleaned on this trip served as furniture and backdrop in my mind for the next several years as I worked with the intelligence materials bearing on Southeast Asia. In subsequent years when I encountered opposition to these "familiarization" tours by clandestine services officers, who generally regarded them at best as shameless junkets and at worst as security hazards to them and their operations—Dick Helms was particularly adept at giving the word "familiarization" a scornful spin—I looked back to my great trip with General Bull and the broad basis for understanding it provided me.

When I got back to South Building I found the Far East staff of the Office of National Estimates deeply involved with the events in Vietnam; especially the shellacking the French were taking at Dien Bien Phu. I soon learned more about the Viet Minh artillery capabilities that Navarre and Cogny, who had been licking their lips with anticipation of a devastating victory, had known nothing about. Indeed, it had been believed both in Paris and in Washington that the communists had neither the guns nor the capability to use them. Guided by this, the French had taken positions down on the flatland at the strategic junction, confident that the Viet Minh would have to mass and attack them frontally in an effort to drive them out.

Instead, the Viet Minh emplaced their guns on the heights above the Dien Bien Phu valley—apparently disassembling them

106

and moving them into position on the backs of men and pack animals—and proceeded to shoot the lights out of the French, ripping up their positions, destroying their stores of materiel, and eventually pocking the airstrip so badly as to deny it to French air forces. The Pentagon intelligence officers were astonished by the skill and sophistication displayed by the Viet Minh gunners in what seemed to be their maiden showing. We were left to speculate about where they got their training—China? the USSR?—and whether foreign advisers were present with the gun crews as they pulled the lanyards.

In more recent years, following the American resignation of purpose and the inglorious departure from Vietnam—abandoning Cam Ranh Bay, a highly sophisticated base worth a thousand fortunes, the U.S. ambassador and his staff scrambling into helicopters lifting off the roof of the besieged embassy as dozens of forsaken loyal Vietnamese allies sought futilely to cling to the struts and undercarriages—I have found it interesting to compare our acceptance of those events with our feelings about the French when they departed not long after the defeat at Dien Bien Phu. It was clear at the time that the French army had not been defeated in Vietnam. Despite the loss of a battle the forces were still intact and the professional army about as battle-worthy as before. But the French will in Paris had been defeated, and the French government ordered its army to pack up and come home. Something similar happened to the United States just about twenty years later.

But the circumstances for the two nations were fundamentally different and, to my mind, less complimentary to the Americans. The French were after all a colonial power. At a time when the anticolonial tides of history were running strong, they were seeking to quell a political revolution under brilliant leadership that was amply supported by external powers. The result was painfully obvious and presumably should have served as an exemplar to us: regular military forces cannot subdue a countryside crawling with highly motivated, revolution-minded irregular fighters. Regular forces can sustain themselves in such a situation and can move freely about in tight concentrations, but they cannot secure the villages and the rural population from the terror and eventual dominance of the revolutionary guerrillas.

By contrast to the French basic purpose, the American intent in Vietnam was not colonial domination. Viewed on a global basis our purpose was to draw a line against the spread of communist-controlled movements, a doctrine we had applied successfully in Italy and Greece and was then—and I would assume remains, despite some recent faltering—a cornerstone of U.S. foreign policy.

As this policy was applied to Vietnam, it consisted of full support for the noncommunist government, which drew its strength from the southern, and as yet undominated, half of the country. For ideological purity, from the American point of view, it would have been ideal for this government of the south to be staunchly democratic and as free from corruption as the municipal governments of, say, Chicago or Jersey City. Alas, it was not. The noncommunist government of South Vietnam was rigorously true to ancient Vietnamese tradition, established centuries before the arrival of the French and reverted to upon their departure; it was a mandarin-styled oligarchy where bribery and corruption played their normal, institutionalized roles in the oriental scheme of things.

Still, the task of halting the advance of international communism need not automatically entail an effort to establish American-style democracies. One would hope that to try to do so might be perceived as unduly complicating an already formidable undertaking. Also, one would think it could have been possible for the Americans to provide enough military and economic support to sustain the noncommunist government while that government pursued in its own fashion the task of persuading its population that established Vietnamese values and traditions were preferable to the alien values of Marxism. Such a task could well have taken several decades. Even then it might not have been successful, but this, of course, we will never know because it was not tried.

Many factors contributed to produce an Americanization of the anticommunist effort in Vietnam but surely very prominent

108

among them was American impatience. Lyndon Johnson epitomized this American failing, with his prototypical talk of "nailing the coonskin on the wall" and his pouring of massive forces into the battle so that the boys could be home by Christmas. Inevitably, the anticommunist struggle in Vietnam became an American venture, so perceived by ourselves, the world at large, the leadership in Hanoi, and—most fatally—by the leadership in Saigon. We took over their cause and made it impossible for them to succeed with their own populace even if they had had the capability to do so. As a consequence, we were perceived as having assumed the colonial role formerly held by the French. Hanoi saw it that way, as did the American Left, and, most unfortunately, vast numbers of American people.

The final irony, it seems to me, in this tragic episode in American foreign policy is that the proximate cause of the precipitate American departure from Vietnam was remarkably similar to the event that caused the French abandonment. For the French, it was Dien Bien Phu; for us, it was the Tet Offensive. In neither instance was there a military defeat so great that it required surrender. In both there was a final collapse of will at home. What makes this even more ironic is that there was no defeat at all for the Americans, as Dien Bien Phu had been for the French. There was instead the *perception* of defeat by the U.S. media that was purveyed to the American public. Unfortunately, by this time the U.S. military leadership in Saigon and Washington had so heavily undermined its credibility that no amount of truthful protest could prevail. And yet, I firmly believe that any fair-minded historian, who looks at Viet Cong objectives in this blitz offensive, their total failure to achieve those goals, and the heavy losses they suffered in cadre and carefully wrought networks, will conclude that the Tet Offensive was a communist defeat. It was a desparate all-out gamble in which they gained tremendous surprise and great psychological advantage. But for them it was a solid tactical and military defeat. Not, however, to the *New York Times* and CBS.

109

Singapore

6

Not only Vietnam engaged the Far East staff as the year 1953 dwindled to a close and 1954 came rolling in. Other matters on which we were expected to have answers included: Would Indonesia's first postindependence national elections be held before the country sank into bankruptcy? Would the well-nigh continuous artillery fire and counterfire between Quemoy, Matsu, and mainland China erupt into full-scale war? Would the Huk rebellion in the Philippines be quelled or break out anew? Would the next turn of the wheel within the military oligarchy of Thailand bring forth a strong man from the growing ranks of U.S.-trained, democratic-minded young colonels?

In retrospect I came to realize that the Eisenhower administration marked a golden era for national intelligence estimates. President Eisenhower ran an orderly, highly structured shop. There was a great deal of military spirit in the administration's staff work that derived both from the World War II service of many officials and Eisenhower's own work habits. Estimates had an acknowledged role, a designated place, in the process of formulating national policy and strategy. When policy papers were submitted to the National Security Council they were accompanied by an NIE that described and analyzed the potential threat—or opportunity—presented therein to U.S. security interests, analyzed its dynamics, and essayed some prediction as to the pace at which it might proceed and its likely outcome. Given the orderly, steady, even progression with which the NSC took on these policy deliberations, there was time to schedule an estimate a month or two before it was needed, time to form fully developed, rounded intelligence judgments. There was even time in this process to alert intelligence collectors—diplomats, spies, and technical devices operators—that information bearing upon certain questions should be given priority attention. It was a highly rational, precise, efficient system, like finely meshed gears turning smoothly in light machine oil, a planner's dream come true.

Cynics may point out with some accuracy that remarkably few policy decisions emerged from this elegant system or that when they did little action followed, unless perchance the decision was consonant with the interests and ideas of the headstrong secretary of state, John Foster Dulles. But that was no fault of the system, which was itself a thing of beauty. I might add as postscript that the contrast between Eisenhower policy-making procedures and those of the Kennedys could not have been greater. The stately progression of NSC policy papers, one by one, week by week, gave way suddenly and without transition to the rollicking Kennedy style where policy-making most resembled something like a pickup touch football game crossed with a Harvard seminar. There was plenty of participation and consultation, but many of the participants were outsiders from Wall Street and the campuses. It was all so spontaneous and so loosely organized that there was no designated role for intelligence. One man's facts or his judgments were as good as another's, and intelligence had to knock on the door to get in. That realization out at Langley headquarters caused us to adjust our approach to providing high-level intelligence, but now I am getting ahead of myself.

112

As the year 1954 moved forward I became increasingly engaged in an exciting prospect. I was going to Singapore as a Department of State officer to serve in the consulate general. On my return to Washington with General Bull, I had written the mandatory trip report, and in it I had suggested that an officer from the estimative side of CIA, loaned to the State Department for a two-year tour, could make a contribution in regional understanding for both State and the Agency. When I saw my suggestion taking root in the bureaucratic soil I quickly nominated myself for the job.

The deal was closed one morning in a corridor of South Building. Robert Amory, Jr., then deputy director for intelligence, former Harvard professor, and a lean, hard-driving man with a hawk-like profile, came striding toward me. "Tell me," he said, "about this Singapore thing. Do you really want it, or is Sherm Kent trying to get you out of the way?"

"No. I really want it. I think something useful can be done there."

"Okay, it's yours." And Amory strode off.

My family and I tumbled out of a KLM Constellation onto Singapore's Palamar Airport tarmac one August afternoon in 1954. Instead of the welcoming delegation General Bull and I had found the year before, we were met by an overplump, purse-lipped secretary who escorted us to the comfortably seedy Sea View Hotel facing Singapore Harbor.

After Rosemary and I had got settled and the children bedded we took a brief stroll in the vicinity of the Sea View. On a side street we passed a string of sidewalk stalls, blazingly lighted by acetylene lamps, where street merchants were selling aromatic fried foods, bananas, pineapples, and scarlet rambutans. As we returned we walked across the stone esplanade before the entrance of the Sea View Hotel and looked out across the sea wall toward scores of freighters, fishing boats, and coastal junks, the lights on their gently swaying masts twinkling in the sea breeze like fireflies. All at once the realization was vivid: we had left behind the demure suburbs and formal buildings of Washington. This was exotic

Singapore, a city that epitomized the Orient. Resonances of Joseph Conrad, Sir Stamford Raffles, and Somerset Maugham ring from the name: Singapore. It was my very good fortune to be there. Few Americans have the opportunity to live—not visit—*live* overseas, and fewer still can live in a place so richly endowed with material pleasures and cultural variety. I was certain it was all going to work out just fine.

Daily life in Singapore for my wife and my, by then, three sons was as thoroughly delightful as foreseen, but it would be hard to say whose daily round had been more greatly changed by the flight from one side of the world to the other. The younger boys, two and four, suddenly found themselves under the constant supervision of a pear-shaped Chinese *amah*, Ah Yuen, with gold teeth, black-bottomed and white-topped pajamas, whose final command of the day before tucking them into bed was, "Washee tee' velly clickly!" At this point the two cherubs, scrubbed, fed, and petted, were turned over to their well-rested parents for a bedtime story.

The oldest boy, thirteen, no longer took a yellow Fairfax County bus to school but instead was driven several miles in our black Ford sedan by Talib bin Muhammed, the Malay *syce*, to St. Andrew's School for Asian Boys where he joined a handful of other "Europeans" amid a dominant population of Chinese and Indian boys. The Indian master who taught English possessed a mastery of the tongue several grades inferior to our Stephen's, which caused moments of considerable friction. Otherwise, the instruction was good and challenging for Stephen. He responded by rising to the rank of "Number One Boy" in his class, an honor that created deep chagrin in the diligent Chinese lad who had previously held the title. The daily ride to and from school soon made Stephen and Talib fast friends, and Stephen acquired a passable "kitchen Malay."

Rosemary no longer cooked our meals, cleaned the house, did the laundry, and tended little boys from sunup to sundown. Instead, she needed only to make out menus and supervise the performance

114

of Chang, the cookboy; Ah Yuen, the *amah;* and Wee Wat, Chang's wife and our laundress. This left time for bridge or mah jong with British, Chinese, and American ladies or, even more delightful for her, time for shopping. Singapore in the midfifties was a paradise for shoppers. Every choice article produced in Europe, Asia, or America was available. Beach Road was a dazzling array of shops selling gold-embroidered saris, petal-thin Chinese bowls, and other elegant creations by tradition-trained Indian and Chinese artisans. Rosemary who, for the most part, shopped rather than bought, soon became the leading American expert on where treasures were to be found.

As for me, suddenly deprived of a meadow to mow, a garden to weed, firewood to cut, and an automobile to wash and keep serviced, I turned to the Royal Singapore Golf Club for release of untapped physical energy. The Royal Singapore, or "Bukit Timah," the Malay name that described its location, was a proper British club to the last inch. Palm trees had been ruthlessly exterminated along the fairways, and the whole landscape groomed to give it as English and as nontropical a look as possible. The effect was mostly successful. Standing on a gentle hill looking down on a lake-like reservoir you could imagine yourself in England. But the effect was severely diminished when trees along the fairways suddenly sprouted plate-sized lavender blossoms or, as happened once, when two Chinese came trotting across a fairway with a bamboo pole slung over their shoulders on which was lashed a six-foot python.

Decorum at the club was strict. I once saw the club secretary admonish a young Frenchman, a visitor wearing shorts cut in the French style up to the crotch, for "improper dress." Never mind that the wide-bottomed British shorts displayed in living color and anatomical detail the wearer's "family jewels" when seated and caused ladies with more modesty than curiosity to look hastily away.

My immediate reaction to being attended by a staff of five servants was embarrassed resentment. Surely I could drive my own car. "No," I was advised, "if you do the *syces* will slash your tires when you park at receptions." Another insight into Asian techniques for job protection came when I inquired about the size of the household staff. This, it seemed, was established by the cookboy, the major domo, who inspected the size and luxury of the house and set the correct number of servants. To have a lesser number would cause such loss of face that good servants would not take the job.

I met face in another aspect when Chang, just before the weekend marking Chinese New Year, a time of great celebration, asked for Talib to drive him, a live chicken, and other ingredients for a feast to his house. "Talib has the afternoon off," I told Chang. "I will drive you myself."

Chang's broad face took on a look of horror, and a gold tooth gleamed in a grimace. "Oh, no, Master! Chinese boy see out window my house, and they *laugh!*" The only solution, it seemed, was to send Chang by taxi.

Social life in Singapore was intense. Shortly after our arrival we began to be inundated with cocktail and dinner party invitations. At first it was exhilarating, a party virtually every night, but Rosemary and I found it unnatural and quickly tired of it. "Three nights a week is my absolute limit," I declared. "More than that, and I grow surly."

We also reserved Sunday for the boys, whom we usually took to Changi Beach for a picnic. When we returned home in late afternoon, sandy, hot, and overexposed to the equatorial sun, I experienced a moment that to me expressed the greatest luxury I have ever known. We simply climbed out of the hot car, left the doors wide open and the picnic remains in the trunk, turned the boys over to the *amah*, and walked into the house to a cool shower. The servants swarmed out to the car and relieved us of the wearisome aftermath of a family picnic in the sun.

The house I found for my family was a long bungalow sited on a slight hill overlooking a Malay *kampong*. It happened to be the most fortunate house in Singapore. This I learned from its

116

owner, a Chinese spice merchant, who had been so informed by a Chinese geomancer who had searched the island for the house with that honor. My round-faced landlord explained the reasons. The house faced north, toward China, and it was embraced by the surrounding hills that held it in the bosom of the earth. As I picked my way with great care down the steps of the spice merchant's office—steps that were of irregular height, some shallow, some steep, in order to trip any evil spirits who might think to climb them—I congratulated myself again on my good fortune.

That first afternoon, as we sat in the living room with a drink before dinner, Rosemary and I marveled once again over the delightful strangeness of our new home. The entire front wall of the living room and dining room was a set of glass doors that folded back on either side. With no screens, the outside and our living room became one. An occasional insect found its way in where it quickly became a snack for the suction-cup-footed little lizards, *chi-chas* that roamed the walls and ceiling. Passing on the road some fifty yards away an Indian boy drove an ox pulling a high-wheeled cart stacked high with hay, and behind came another boy carrying a switch and herding eight or ten cattle. Now and then a batik-clad Malay woman came walking out of the grove of palms that shrouded the *kampong* across the road. We were truly half a world away from Virginia and Fairfax County.

Word came out from Washington one day that Robert Amory, Jr., CIA deputy director of intelligence, would be attending the forthcoming Southeast Asian Treaty Organization (SEATO) conference in Bangkok to provide intelligence support for the U.S. delegation and that I was to join him in Bangkok for this task. Bob Amory and I met at the U.S. Embassy in Bangkok and were chauffeured to our temporary lodgings in the guest house of the dominant Thai political party. We shared a huge, opulent, marble-floored room with a twenty-foot ceiling and filled with clusters of bulging and musty overstuffed furniture and with two single beds, each shrouded with mosquito netting. The bathroom was the size of a generous American hotel room and featured a set of marble steps that led into a tank-sized bathtub, deep enough for a man to stand with water up to his waist and long enough for quick laps. Tea and the morning paper were brought to us on huge silver trays borne by barefooted little men in white trousers and jackets.

My work during the three-day conference was easy. I read the background cables from Washington each morning and selected half a dozen for the daily briefing of the U.S. delegation. Amory and I usually discussed the situations he was to cover, exchanging judgments and filling in details. Usually my role was to provide longer-range insights and projections, often restraining Amory's tendency to overreact and overdramatize. When it came to detailed information about situations and developments all around the globe Bob Amory was hard to match. He worked very hard at it, arriving at his DDI office in Washington at 7:30 A.M. and reading all the traffic he could lay his hands on. He used to terrorize Sherman Kent and other members of the Board of National Estimates with his superior grasp of facts and details of foreign developments, but the staff people found him easy to handle, fun, stimulating and receptive to reasoned analysis, to wit: "Yes, I agree that Prince Sihanouk's recent measures smack of medieval feudalism, but you must recognize that he has neutralized all the opposition forces in Cambodia with these steps." Amory, who had been charging full tilt, eyes blazing and nostrils flaring, would listen intently, expression fixed and eyes boring into the speaker, and then would say, "I see what you mean. Good point."

At one of these sessions, Amory remarked to me, "I think you're doing a fine job down there in Singapore. You've caught the eye of Allen Dulles. In our staff meetings now he asks, 'What does Jack Smith in Singapore say about this?' " This was cheering news, but it led me to ponder how reputations are formed in organizations like CIA. What I had been doing in Singapore was no different from what I had done for some time in Washington. If anything, my work was more peripheral. But because I was out at the end of the line, so to speak, a solitary figure detached from the mass of hard-working people in Washington, my voice was heard and identified and listened to. There was a lesson here, and I never ceased to point it out to junior officers later in my career. Bob Amory concluded our talk by telling me that when I came back to Washington he wanted me to work with him in CIA as his National Security Council assistant. This was a prestigious job, highly sought after in Amory's directorate, the DDI, and I accepted promptly.

The SEATO conference of 1955 had little to offer in terms of substantive accomplishments, but it did have a brilliant cast of characters: John Foster Dulles headed the U.S. delegation; Anthony Eden, the British; Henri Bonnet, the French; and Richard Casey, the Australian. Bonnet's contribution to international understanding was to insist on speaking only in French, which had to be pains-takingly interpreted for the Pakistanis, the Thai, and—not least—the Americans, while all the other participants spoke English, or at least idiosyncratic versions thereof. But it remained for the representatives of two leading British Commonwealth countries, the United Kingdom and Australia, to put on the only really diverting performance.

It came during the last session, which was devoted to producing the conference communiqué. Sir Richard Casey, it developed, wanted the communiqué to name communist aggression as the raison d'être and principal target of SEATO, and he wished to have this made explicit. Anthony Eden, on the other hand, wished to make the statement applicable to all forms of international aggression, offering among other arguments that he did not wish to give the communist movement the recognition and satisfaction that might derive from being singled out. The two elegant statesmen, similar in dark theatrical handsomeness, suave demeanor, and well-bred speech, feinted and sparred in quiet modulated voices like two sleek and well-mannered Siamese cats. It was a delightful performance, the very model of sophisticated diplomacy. Into this drawing-room scene barged the twang and heavy-shouldered thrust of the American secretary of state, John Foster Dulles. Lounging sideways on one hip, his large beak-nosed face dark red and aggressively unattractive—I once saw Dulles and J. Edgar Hoover sitting side by side in President Eisenhower's briefing room, Hoover's face a reddish purple, similar to Dulles's in that it strongly resembled a snapping turtle, and I thought to myself that I was looking at the two ugliest men in America—he announced in condescendingly insulting tones that he saw no reason not to name the communists. If they were the foe, why not say so?

Casey bowed his head slightly in recognition of this blast of support while Anthony Eden got to his feet, unruffled, and proceeded to make an exceedingly graceful 180-degree turn. He would prefer to make the statement more broadly applicable to aggressors of every stripe, but if there was a consensus in the conference in the other direction he certainly did not wish to stand in the way. He smiled politely at Dulles and sat down. Whereupon the American secretary turned his heavy head around and bestowed an exaggerated, owlish wink upon the rest of the American delegation in the row behind him. In the next row behind the Americans sat the members of the British delegation who exchanged sardonic glances with one another while I winced at this oafishness.

I also attended the SEATO conference the following year in Karachi. Only two things stand out about the meeting in that tawdry city. One, the sanitation in the hotel where I was staying was so deplorable that my friends in the embassy urged me to brush my teeth in Scotch whiskey instead of the "boiled" water offered by the management. The other was a trip up the Khyber Pass in the company of Prime Minister Casey and Prime Minister Holyoake of New Zealand as guests of the Pakistani government. At the top of the pass, where the Pakistani and Afghan border runs, we had lunch in the flag-bedecked mess hall of the Khyber Rifles. For years afterward, this memorable and exotic occasion was my stopper in verbal jousts with my friend and colleague, the ebullient Robert Komer. "Ah, yes," I would say when he threatened to get out of hand, "puts me in mind of the time I had lunch with the Khyber Rifles."

Back to Headquarters

7

I found when I returned to CIA headquarters in September 1956 that I had been traduced by some behind-my-back bureaucratic maneuvering. The NSC assistant job that Robert Amory, Jr., had promised me when we were together in Bangkok had been appropriated by Bob Komer. Komer had gone to our immediate boss, Sherman Kent, and had persuaded him not only that he should be relieved of the onerous ONE chief of staff job but that it was my turn to take it over. All of us on the staff detested the job. Despite its title you were chief of nothing, merely a straw boss among your peers, and required through guile and persuasion to organize their work and make it responsive to the views and whims of the Board of National Estimates. Thankless at best.

Still, I felt no particular animosity toward Bob Komer. All of us who had worked with him over the years viewed with mingled amusement and affection his brash, driving energy and unadulterated chutzpah. We also respected his mind, his ability to generate novel ideas and insights that came tumbling out with blinding rapidity. I often felt that I should keep a bushel basket by my desk to collect these Komerish concepts as they cascaded forth and then later, after he had gone and the tumult had subsided, sort them over, throw out the many outrageous ones and keep the few gems.

So I resigned myself to the inevitable—Komer was right; it *was* my turn—and hoped that my tenure would be short. It turned out to be remarkably short. Within a few months I was made Allen Dulles's representative on an NSC staff, which operated in the Pentagon under the auspices of the Joint Chiefs of Staff, a post that required the incumbent to be a member of the Board of National Estimates. It was an unexpected ascension, being elevated from the staff to the exalted board, but one I attributed merely to being in the right place at the right time.

To diverge briefly, I have always been fascinated by this "right place–right time" aspect of professional careers. I am almost convinced that it is the most important element in advancement in large, structured organizations. I have already mentioned the anomaly of my coming to high-level attention while performing in a role less central to the main effort of the CIA than I performed in Washington. As for the Pentagon job, it is true I had certain qualifications for working with military officers because of my National War College experience. Several others had that qualification as well, however, but I was there and readily available. The usual rejoinder to this line of thought is that one must have the required capability for the job that fortune has dropped in your lap. True enough, but in a large organization there usually are a number of equally qualified people who simply are not at "the r.p.–r.t." Not long ago, I discovered that none other than General Ulysses S. Grant shared my view. Musing over the death of the benefactor who had got him his West Point appointment, Congressman Haber, "one of the ablest men Ohio ever produced," General Grant speculated that if not for his untimely death in the Mexican War, Haber would likely have become president and made Grant a staff officer, perhaps in the U.S. Army Pay Department. "Neither of these speculations is unreasonable, and they are mentioned to show how little men control their own destiny" (*Memoirs* 2 vols. [New York: C. L. Webster, 1885] vol. I, p. 103).

The task of the NSC staff to which I was assigned in the Pentagon was to make an annual appraisal of the relative strengths of the United States and the Soviet Union in an all-out nuclear war. We worked full-time for a year at preparing our report, which was delivered orally to the president and his National Security Council. My colleagues consisted of two each Army and Air Force colonels, two Navy captains, and a Marine colonel. A four-star Marine general headed the staff; an Air Force brigadier general was his deputy. As the only civilian, I was sometimes regarded askance, especially by the brigadier general, a hard-charging former Strategic Air Command officer who seemed to work day and night to maintain the image he felt appropriate to a SAC commander. I once tried to meet his highly vocal condescension toward civilians by openly confessing my faults. "Not only that," I told him, "but I *married* a civilian and *all* my children are civilians!" I had the uneasy feeling later that this sarcasm had skimmed by him as though he had been brushed by a feather.

In readying the report, we had to amass the figures on the weaponry of the armed forces of the two putative opponents and their estimated effectiveness. My job was to provide the latest CIA judgments on these matters. We also made a number of trips to inspect U.S. forces during their training exercises. The most memorable of these for me was a visit to the Sixth Fleet in the Mediterranean during a NATO exercise. Our group was flown from Naples out to the carrier, *Franklin Delano Roosevelt*, by a propellor-driven transport termed a COD ("carrier on-deck delivery"). The *FDR* was maintaining radio silence during the exercise, so our plane flew with only the guidance that she was somewhere in the vicinity of Crete. When the *FDR* was sighted she looked from our altitude about the size of a canoe, but we circled down, hit her broad deck with a bang, and experienced that astonishingly rapid deceleration as the dangling hook caught the restraining wire and stopped us. The passenger seats all faced to the rear, and my head and shoulders were pinned to the back of the seat for what seemed a very long time. I could only imagine what it must seem to the pilot and copilot facing forward.

The *FDR* conducted simulated night-bombing attacks that night, and all night long the deck over my bunk banged and the ship shuddered as the incoming bombers returned to their nest. Early in the evening we had stood on the operations bridge overlooking the flight deck and watched the bombers as they were launched over the bow by the steam catapults, each time dipping down almost to the water as they came off the deck. When they returned, one by one, they looked enormous as they approached the fantail, far too large for the angled deck. A ship's officer standing beside us said, just before the plane slammed onto the deck, "First one who ducks is a coward."

It was that night that I learned that all three of the innovations that made carrier operations feasible with jet aircraft were British inventions: The steam catapult essential to get jets airborne, the mirror landing system ("the meatball," the pilots call it) that provides precise final guidance, and the angled flight deck that enables a jet, with its slower acceleration, to bounce and take off again if the hook does not catch the wire. An astonishing fact considering that the total British experience in aircraft carrier operations is a miniscule fraction of ours.

I also came that night to the firm conviction that aircraft carrier operations, especially heavy jet bomber operations, and even more especially nighttime operations under real combat conditions, are sheer circus dare-devilry. You must imagine the pilot of a two-engine jet bomber coming in to land on a deck of a ship that is rising and falling ten to twenty feet in the dark. No lights are on anywhere on the ship, but the man in the cockpit locates the red "meatball" in the mirror system and tries to keep it in the center of his finder. His engine throttles are set at 85 percent full power. The instant the plane slams onto the deck he opens the throttles wide. He knows that if he hooks successfully he will be thrown violently forward against his restraining harness as his plane comes

124

to a screeching stop within a few feet, an event I liken to a man trying to thread a needle in the dark in the full knowledge that if he succeeds he will take a blow to the jaw. If his hook fails to catch, his plane will continue across the angled deck, dip down toward the sea as it labors to regain full flying speed, and then he has to repeat the process.

I have seen pilots in night training exercises off Mayport, Florida, make three or four vain attempts to get their plane down onto that carrier. One poor lad got his wheels to hit the steel deck on his first try, but the hook bounced and failed to catch, and he went off and on around. The second time he could get his plane no lower than fifteen feet above the deck, and the third time he was at least fifty feet over the ship. After that, he gave up and flew back to Mayport, no doubt a dispirited and shaken young man. When one adds to these inherent difficulties the possibility that in actual combat the bomber might return with damaged control surfaces on the wings or tail or with an engine knocked out, it is easy to come to the conclusion I did that night in 1958.

Our team also made visits to forward SAC bomber bases in Morocco and Spain and inspected the B-47 bombers poised for takeoff on fifteen-minute warning. Later, we toured SAC headquarters in Omaha and inspected the operations room with its high-speed communications net and the dazzling display boards for monitoring combat and the location of SAC planes. From there we were flown out to a Minute Man complex in Montana where we climbed down into the grim, silent silos hiding the sleek weapons. My Air Force colleagues, all with six thousand to eight thousand hours of flying time in the service, shuddered at the thought of a career spent in an underground silo. Because our task required us to be aware of new weapons development, we toured Edwards Air Force Base in California where experimental aircraft are tested and at least a half-dozen research and development facilities of such manufacturers as Lockheed, Aero-jet General, and Hewlett-Packard. Some of the concepts the eager and voluble young scientists were offering were a bit wild-eyed. I remember in particular one bearded and bright-eyed researcher who was dreaming of a tiny ion engine that could power a spacecraft once it was in space. His notion was that once free of the atmospheric drag only minute outputs of energy would be needed to accelerate the vehicle. His proposed ion engine developed such tiny outputs that he felt it necessary to develop a new term to describe them. His term was "mouse-pharts."

After this extensive education in U.S. forces and weaponry, we turned to setting up an elaborate, computerized war game. When the results came in we wrote our report, and after a week of daily rehearsals, we crossed the Potomac to the White House— my military friends uniformed and beribboned—and presented it to President Eisenhower and his assembled strategic advisers. It was a stark report. To be sure, if one totted up the losses each side suffered, it could be said that the Soviet Union's loss was greater than ours. But the devastation inflicted on both countries, as described by the report, was terrible. It was my task to present orally the damage the United States received, the percentage of the civilian population killed, the numbers wounded by burn, blast, or severe radiation, the overloaded medical facilities, the smashed and useless communication system, and the rest of the horrors. My teammates remarked that through it all President Eisenhower never took his eyes off my face. At the end he asked me a question— I can no longer remember what it was, but it was a thoughtful one—and thanked me gently for my answer.

In the discussion that took place with his advisers after our report was concluded, I noted that his remarks were direct and intelligent. With my English professor's ear I listened for the fractured presidential syntax the *Washington Post* was gleefully reporting daily. As the sentences emerged from the president's lips they did not sound broken or bent. Like most of us, Eisenhower in conversation spoke in ellipses and fragments. Written verbatim his remarks perhaps would have disclosed imperfect syntax. In direct conversation they sounded like the speech of an intelligent, articulate man.

Shortly after my two-year tour on the NSC committee staff, I returned to the Office of National Estimates as a full-time member of the board. My stint in the Pentagon had provided another string to my bow; I was now qualified to take a role in the preparation of the national intelligence estimates on Soviet strategic forces. My first involvement came with the famous "missile gap" estimate. I remember sitting down with the chief drafter of the estimate to go over the evidence with him. It was very skimpy. Extrapolating from the data and from what we understood about missile manufacture, we made a *capabilities* estimate. The estimate carefully stated its number in those terms; it was what the USSR *could* do, not what it had done. Unfortunately, as we learned then and experienced many times later, many of our readers ignored what seemed to them an academic distinction and took the number that emerged as a flat statement of existing fact.

There was another aspect that skewed that number in the wrong direction. The Air Force came in with an estimated number several times higher than ours, standard Air Force practice in the 1950s that became traditional over the next two decades. Theirs, as usual, was the worst-case stance, quite defensible in military tradition in determining what is the worst threat the enemy can pose. The CIA approach was to search out the *most likely*, not the worst possible, and then leave it to the president and his advisers to decide whether it was better to prepare defenses for the conceivable worst, the most likely, or something in between. In this instance we were at a disadvantage because the evidence was so skimpy. We, a bunch of nonuniformed civilians, were confronting the service that had the greatest experience and technical background in the missile field. Indeed, at that time CIA was just developing the expertise and technical knowledge that later made us more than a match for the Air Force or any other service. Under the circumstances in 1959, we accepted a higher number than our best judgment suggested was the right one. The Air Force, characteristically, dissented even from this number and took one several times higher.

127

As it later became evident, the CIA "hunch" number was much too high, and the Air Force number was preposterous. This, in essence, is the story of the missile gap. In his presidential campaign against Richard Nixon in 1960, John F. Kennedy exploited this "deficiency" in a successful race. Later, in office, he learned the inaccuracy of the claim and abandoned it. Richard Nixon, on the other hand, believed that he had been blindsided by CIA in a deliberate effort to help Kennedy win the election. He never forgot or forgave, as we learned to our sorrow after he became president in 1968.

My Pentagon experience and new-found expertise—"demi-expertise" would be more accurate—in strategic military matters led me into a little venture that gave me a short burst of glory among U.S. military leaders. *Foreign Affairs*, a quarterly magazine read religiously by scholars of international affairs and professionals in national security organizations, published in 1959 a piece by Professor Albert Wohlstetter that created a considerable stir. Titled "The Delicate Balance of Deterrence," it sought to demonstrate that the USSR could overwhelm U.S. strategic forces in a sudden surprise attack. The article struck me as highly theoretical and academic, thoroughly out of touch with hard military realities that then and now underlie all aspects of a possible U.S.-Soviet nuclear exchange, especially the likelihood of a surprise attack. Still, I was not inclined to tilt against academic windmills until I was assailed by one of our consultants, a Columbia University professor of Soviet affairs, who rejected my comments on the Wohlstetter article as uninformed, assuring me that I did not have the thorough understanding of the matter that Wohlstetter did.

That triggered a response, and I sat down at my typewriter at home one Sunday morning and wrote a critique. I began with the difficulties of obtaining total surprise in modern warfare. I had been in the SAC underground command center in Omaha when an exercise had been run, and I had observed the command go out to the bombers on standby alert to take off when word came in that fires had mysteriously broken out in the paint lockers of two or three SAC bomber bases, incidents that could have been sabotage designed to distract those bases prior to enemy attacks.

I also knew how sensitive the U.S. intelligence system was to signs of tension in the Soviet Union: indications of unusual traffic, the sudden return of Soviet ambassadors from their posts around the world, movements of troops, ships, and aircraft. When any of these developments are observed, U.S. forces go on a heightened state of alert, and the reaction time to surprise attack is reduced to its lowest possible time. To succeed on the scale Professor Wohlstetter was projecting, the Soviet attack would have to come totally out of the blue, unprovoked, during a period of serenity and calm.

I then tried to describe the task facing a Soviet military leader who had been charged by his political superiors with knocking out U.S. strategic forces with minimal damage to the USSR. Beginning with his own intercontinental ballistic missiles (ICBMs), I cited the figures he must use for reliability and accuracy. The Soviet commander would know that when the button was pushed not all his missiles would fire. This was the factor of reliability; a working figure with liquid-propelled missiles in 1960 might be 85 percent. So out of every one hundred missiles, fifteen might fizzle on their launch pads. Then he would consider accuracy. At that time a working assumption might be that only half of the missiles that got off their pads would fall within a circle several miles in diameter around their target while the other half would fall outside that circle. In other words, even given perfect surprise he would have to assume that some U.S. missiles, possibly a substantial number, would remain unscathed and would fire in retaliation.

I then tried to tot up how many nuclear weapons the Soviet commander could expect his country to receive in a U.S. retaliatory attack. Let X be the number of surviving U.S. missiles. Then he would turn to the SAC bombers, possibly off and winging toward the USSR before the first Soviet missile landed, sweeping over Soviet terrain in a coordinated, sophisticated attack combining low-level runs, saturation formations, and standoff air-to-surface missiles. His air-defense system would respond and would shoot many of the bombers out of the sky. But *some would get through.* Trying to estimate how many, he would apply the kill probability his test engineers had provided him. If he were very optimistic, he might use a figure of 90 percent, but having done so, he would realize that 90 percent of several hundred leaves a disturbing number of U.S. bombers, each carrying nuclear bombs amounting to tens of megatons, that would reach their assigned targets, not to mention the number of shot-down bombers whose weapons might detonate on impact. Next he would have to consider the U.S. submarines stationed off the coasts of Europe, firing immediately when the message came that the United States was under attack. And after that the carrier-based bombers on the Sixth Fleet in the Mediterranean, and the attack bombers at forward bases in Germany would be brought into play.

The result of these reckonings, I suggested in my paper, would be the realization that under any realistic circumstance the Soviet Union would suffer extensive damage, probably amounting to hundreds of megatons, even after mounting the most successful surprise attack it could achieve. I did not cite any exact number, but I stressed the uncertainty the Soviet commander would be confronting. He could not assure his civilian superiors that the damage received would be tolerable.

Of course, the word "tolerable" opens a wide door. What would Soviet leaders regard as tolerable? Back in the late 1950s and early 1960s, when the Cold War was most intense, I have heard men who seemed otherwise sane argue at length whether the USSR would accept the destruction of ten, fifteen, or twenty Russian cities in exchange for a knockout blow against the United States. I never believed for an instant in such a notion. I am convinced the Soviet leaders are far too conscious of the fragility of their hard-won industrial progress and partially modernized society to risk it on a single go-for-broke blow at the United States. The key word here is "risk." Risk implies some uncertainty, and great uncertainty is what a professional military leader must report to his civilian bosses.

Back to Headquarters

My two years' education in the Pentagon on the mechanics of nuclear warfare instilled a deep conviction in me that nearly all discussion of the putative nuclear exchange displays an appalling lack of imagination regarding the blast, blood, and flame involved. Despite the stark photographs of post-attack Hiroshima, most professional strategists adopt a bloodless, theoretical tone in analyzing the equations of the exchange. I have listened to Air Force targeteers speak of patterns in "laying down" nuclear weapons that were reminiscent only of medieval scholastics discussing those proverbial angels and heads of pins. To be sure, Hiroshima was a flimsy Japanese city, but also, to be sure, the weapon involved was a mere twenty kilotons, a firecracker beside a megaton bomb or warhead. Moreover, we are considering not one nuclear weapon but *hundreds*, yes, *thousands*.

I am persuaded that the detonation of only one or two megaton weapons anywhere along the northeastern corridor of the United States would constitute a far greater catastrophe than any hurricane, earthquake, or other disaster this country has ever experienced. It would paralyze our highly integrated industrial/technical society by smashing its communications and its power grids and by terrorizing the populace. I am equally persuaded that the same number of nuclear detonations in the vicinity of Moscow or Odessa would have a similar or greater effect. To me, therefore, true deterrence in the nuclear age means only that the potential adversaries cannot assure themselves they will not receive at least a few retaliatory megaton detonations on their homeland. For that reason, deterrence was not in "delicate balance" in 1959, and it is not today.

My response to Professor Wohlstetter received only limited circulation within CIA, but it came to the attention of Air Force General Charles F. Cabell, then Allen Dulles's deputy. Cabell urged Dulles to give it general circulation, calling it an "excellent and useful" piece in correcting some widespread misunderstandings. Mr. Dulles, characteristically cautious in such matters, pronounced in his best son-of-a-minister manner, "I don't think we want to mount the pulpit on this." General Cabell persevered, however, and got Dulles's permission to distribute it among his military colleagues. As it happened, an annual meeting of top U.S. commanders world-wide was being held in Washington at this time, and General Cabell passed it among them.

Quiet descended for a time then, while I settled into the daily routine of a board member. One day General Cabell called me to his office. Waving an incoming cable, he said, "Admiral Felt at CINCPAC wants you to visit him in Hawaii. He wants you to speak to his staff on the subject of your memorandum." I tried to back away from this invitation, but General Cabell thought it important that I accept. I had been planning a trip to the Far East the following month, so I agreed to include Admiral Felt's CINCPAC headquarters on my itinerary in November.

The meeting in Hawaii was more embarrassing than gratifying. Admiral Felt had assembled his top officers in intelligence and planning, a group of at least twenty-five senior military men (unfortunately there was no member of my National War College class among them to give me the comfort of a familiar face). They all sat expectantly while the alleged savant readied himself to pass out wisdom. To ease my awkwardness, Admiral Felt asked, "Have you written any memorandums lately?" I said no but then proceeded to give a brief summary of the gist of my reply to Professor Wohlstetter's article. I knew I was speaking to the converted; none of the points was new to any of them; in fact, I had been told they had all read a copy of my piece by Admiral Felt's order. After my remarks a desultory discussion occurred that Admiral Felt finally terminated with a question. "Where do you go from here?" I named Tokyo, Hong Kong, and Singapore. "How about having Thanksgiving dinner aboard a carrier with the Seventh Fleet?" I pleaded previous plans. He then insisted that I visit the headquarters of the Seventh Fleet's air wing in Yokuska.

It was in the operations room of PACAF, while I was scanning the target plan of the Seventh Fleet's attack bombers, that I finally understood what lay behind Admiral Felt's invitation to visit CINC-PAC and his air wing. PACAF had a capacity to mount retaliatory

132

air strikes against bases and installations in the Soviet Far East. I had left PACAF out in my accounting of the retaliation a Soviet commander would likely confront following a surprise attack. Admiral Felt wanted to make certain it did not happen in any future memorandums. It was this, not a yearning to hear wisdom from the oracle's lips, that had prompted his cable.

After my Far East trip I resumed my position as the new boy on the Board of National Estimates. It was a joy. As a board member I had absolutely no administrative duties. My sole occupation was to keep myself informed on international affairs and attend meetings where these matters, or papers addressing these matters, were discussed. Participation was voluntary. Some board members characteristically doodled on the yellow pads placed before them by attentive secretaries and said nothing for hours at a time. Others maintained a steady fire of comment, sometimes registering hits, sometimes not.

My day began at 8:30 when I read the CIA daily summary, the successor to Harry Truman's newspaper that I had edited in 1947. I also found on my desk a copy of the *New York Times*, which then, at least, was the most authoritative source of international news. Then came the morning staff meeting at which we heard reports of staff progress on upcoming estimates, discussed haphazardly the morning's news, and were informed about that day's meetings with representatives of State Department and service intelligence agencies. Then came the bulk of a board member's work, attending meetings with the representatives of the intelligence agencies to coordinate the estimates with them, page by page, line by line, word by word. Yes, it was tedious and in the minds of most of the younger members of the office, needless. We tried repeatedly to lift the level of the discussion from the words to the issues. In nearly every estimate there were two, three, or four key issues—especially those concerning the Soviet Union—that needed full airing. But most members of our board, like most people in the general population, could not discuss the issues apart from the exact words in which they were stated. So we debated shades of

133

nuances and loaded words with an agreed meaning that any elementary student of semantics would realize could not be transmitted to the cold reader.

Despite this pedestrian, plodding approach, the issues were eventually discussed, albeit tangentially and inefficiently. Beneath the crotchets and submerged biases of the various board members, like Ray Sontag's theological rejection of the word "limited," lay sound judgment. It must be conceded that over the years the national intelligence estimates produced under the aegis of the Board of National Estimates maintained an extraordinarily high standard of objectivity and accuracy. The government and people of the United States were well served by this institution. Nor were the meetings that I have described as tedious undeviatingly dull. Throughout the day flashes of wit from the likes of Chester Cooper or Sherman Kent would pierce the prosaic solemnity. Sherman, in particular, had this knack; he might, for example, liken the feckless efforts of a certain Southeast Asian government to bring order out of its endemic chaos to "gathering piss with a rake."

I lived the life of a board member for three years. Owing to my two years in Singapore and two in the Pentagon I was most frequently assigned estimates on Far East problems and Soviet advanced weaponry. Two such dissimilar areas provided great intellectual stimuli. They also put me in the front row for observing decision making at the highest level. One time, Allen Dulles asked me to accompany him to an NSC meeting where U.S. policy regarding Taiwan and the future prospects of Chiang Kai-shek's government were to be discussed. We had just completed a new estimate—which I had chaired—on this matter. We had come to a conclusion that was highly uncongenial to the Eisenhower administration, especially to its chief steward for foreign affairs, John Foster Dulles; namely, that the prospects for a successful return to the mainland by the Chiang Kai-shek regime were negligible. In the 1950s Chiang's claim to legitimacy rested solely on the assertion that his was the rightful government of China, having been temporarily displaced by a rebel uprising. He would return

134

to the mainland and resume control. This assertion also was the underpinning for U.S. support of Chiang Kai-shek and denial of recognition to Mao Tse-tung. CIA's judgment that such a return was unlikely could only be viewed as heretical, to say the least.

Still, the discussion in the National Security Council meeting flowed along placidly for a time, owing mostly to the late arrival of John Foster Dulles. President Eisenhower sat at his appointed place in the middle of the long table that dominated the cabinet room. While Allen Dulles read through the briefing paper we had provided him, the president doodled steadily on a small white pad, looking up only as he tore off the finished page and folded it into neat quarters before placing it in his breast pocket. His pink, round face looked serene and untroubled, and his glance more resembled that of an interrupted artist than a general of armies. When the secretary of state at last arrived, his heavy face flushed an angry red, President Eisenhower mildly informed him of the topic of discussion and asked for his view. For answer, John Foster Dulles looked straight at his brother, and said, "I can only imagine, Allen, that the men who wrote this estimate are *dyspeptic!*" Apparently this Victorian pejorative word had more sting within the Dulles family than it did for the rest of us, because Allen Dulles retorted hotly, "They are *not* dyspeptic! They are intelligent, knowledgeable people." Then he stopped. (At a meeting of the Board of National Estimates I, at this point, would have assured everyone that my digestive processes were in good order, but in these lofty realms I held my tongue.) "This is a dangerous paper," said the secretary. "I can only imagine what harm would be done if it were read by our allies in Asia." President Eisenhower looked up from his art work and said mildly, "The idea was to start a discussion, and it seems to have done that."

But the discussion never advanced beyond this point. On the way back to CIA headquarters in the long, black director's limousine, Allen Dulles said, "I still think that's a good paper. My brother is very concerned with other matters at present. I'll have a quiet talk with him about it, sometime." So far as I know, no further

NSC discussion of the matter took place in the Eisenhower years, and my hunch has always been that the junior and usually mild-mannered Allen Dulles never braced his stern, dogmatic brother on the subject.

My first captaincy of an estimate on Soviet advanced weapons was an occasion I had looked forward to eagerly. Having sat helpless for hours stretching into days and weeks while *fainéant* chairmen allowed the discussion to dither and dawdle, I was determined to get things moving and keep them moving. Before the first session with representatives of the other intelligence agencies got under way, however, I began to realize the dimensions of the task: the expectation that the meetings would go on for weeks had become institutionalized. The CIA staff man, our resident expert on Soviet weaponry who had drafted the paper, arrived five minutes late. Then he proceeded to move up and down the conference table shaking hands with his military colleagues, old friends all, like a gentleman entering his club. Then he took off his jacket, hung it carefully on a chair behind him, rolled up his sleeves, poured himself a cup of coffee, and seated himself. But not before I had snapped, "For God's sake, sit down so we can get started!"

The meeting began, and despite my chivying and stern muzzling of the staff man, who always wanted to extend the discussion after agreement had been reached, we made no more than the usual first day's progress. The next was little better as it became blindingly apparent that the lieutenants and majors had been conditioned to have their say on subtle points of diction and word order as well as major substantive matters regarding missile and submarine characteristics. And so the days grew into weeks.

Fairness obliges me to say that a new factor in guided missile warfare, the hardening of missile sites, had introduced problems that made agreement more difficult. To make a site hard, that is through steel and concrete reinforcement to make it impervious to blast less than one hundred pounds per square inch (100 psi), meant that direct missile hits were necessary to destroy the site. The equation was already complicated for calculating how many missiles on launcher ready to fire were necessary to have a 75 percent or greater chance of knocking out a missile site. Missile reliability and accuracy, not to mention precise geodetic siting of both launch pad and target, were the essential elements. Now we were adding hardening, which shrank the target area from, let us say, one mile or less to hundreds of yards or less. This made accuracy even more critical. Relatively small differences in accuracy could raise or lower dramatically the number of missiles necessary to target against a single site.

Since no one seemed to have solid figures on the effect hardening would have on the number of missiles required for each target, we decided to produce an illustrative appendix for the estimate that would give our readers some concept of that effect. We commissioned some statistical analysis providing ranges of missile accuracy and reliability as they played against several levels of hardening. It was all theoretical, but some of the numbers produced were staggering. I remember fifty-six. Fifty-six missiles, according to the computation of one combination of reliability, accuracy, and psi, was the number the Soviets would need on launchers to have a 75 percent chance of destroying one hardened U.S. site.

We put no great store on these theoretical studies but felt they had some value as illustration. The intelligence agency representatives took us at our word, and my board colleagues seemed content to go along. By this time the date for delivering the estimate was drawing near, and I scheduled weekend meetings to make the deadline.

We were in a cleaning-up phase one Saturday morning when suddenly from the back of the room the commanding voice of Admiral Jerauld Wright rang out. Admiral Wright, a fellow board member, was a strikingly handsome, imposing figure, tall, eagle-profiled, and bushy eyebrowed. I had first met him at his Norfolk headquarters as commander in chief of the Atlantic Fleet. Sitting behind his massive desk in Navy whites, his four gold stars gleaming on his shoulder boards, he was at least the equal of General

Douglas MacArthur as the very model of an American proconsul. Presence and command rested on his shoulders along with those four stars.

"RJ!" spoke the admiral. "What does this number fifty-six mean?"

"In the appendix you mean, Admiral? Oh, that's a number for missiles required for each target according to one of the computations."

"Well, I don't believe it."

I chuckled. "I'm not sure I believe it either, Admiral. It's just an illustration."

"Well, I don't agree with it. We ought to take it out."

I shuddered. This was getting serious. The appendix had been reviewed by the board and the intelligence representatives, approved, and put to bed. We had the finish line in sight after three weeks of haggling. This was no time to reopen things already approved.

"But we all reviewed it last week, Admiral, and passed it."

"I didn't notice it then. I don't think it's right, and it ought to come out."

No need to give a play-by-play of the ensuing encounter. In another minute I was in hot dispute with Admiral Wright with no holds barred. In the middle of a fierce riposte, there came a knock at the door, and a secretary put in her head. "Mr. Dulles would like to see Admiral Wright."

The admiral got to his feet and stalked out of the room. I sat trying to pull myself together and get the meeting back on track. In less than a minute, Admiral Wright opened the door again. "May I see you for a moment, RJ?"

Expecting the worst and ready to resume the argument, I met him in the hallway. "I don't like it, but if you think that number is all right there, RJ, you leave it in."

In my astonishment I could only say, "Thank you, Admiral." He strode off toward Allen Dulles's office, and I felt certain that the obstinacy of the youngest member of the board would be mentioned.

Back to Headquarters

The next morning, Sunday, I met Mr. Dulles as I came into the building. "Good morning, Jack. How's the estimate coming?"

"Pretty well, Mr. Dulles. We've got a few things left to iron out, but I think we'll make it. Finish today."

"Good. Jerry Wright tells me you're doing a fine job as chairman."

I ought not to have been surprised by such magnanimity from a man of Admiral Wright's dimension, but I confess I was. My admiration for him grew tenfold, and in years to come we developed a friendship I treasured.

This ought to have ended the saga of the unfortunate number, fifty-six, but when we were reviewing the paper with Allen Dulles before final approval his glance fell on fifty-six. "What does this number here mean?"

I explained. Dulles protested, "But I don't understand why each time you fire a missile you don't have a 50-50 chance of hitting the target. If you miss once you ought to get it next time."

Allen Dulles was a man of wide and varied talents, but he clearly was no statistician. He was, however, a leader who placed confidence in his subordinates. Though visibly unconvinced, he accepted our assurances and passed it by. This brought to a close my first outing as chairman of an important estimate and gave me fair warning of similar vicissitudes yet to come.

My stay on the Board of National Estimates lasted until 1962, and it is pertinent to observe that I have made no mention of two events in this period that are usually regarded as cataclysmic for CIA: the shoot-down of Gary Powers in his U-2 and the Bay of Pigs. The truth is that they made only a minor impact upon my work and my concept of CIA's role. Why this is so casts considerable light upon the internal structure of an organization like CIA. Without rehashing the course of the events themselves, which have been intensively scrutinized and discussed, it might be interesting to consider how they appeared to us in the estimates side of the Agency.

139

The eventual loss of the U-2 as an intelligence collector had been expected. Although the aircraft at its operational altitude was thought to be reasonably safe from the current surface-to-air missiles or fighters, it was assumed that more advanced weapons would someday demonstrate a capacity to knock the U-2 down, most likely through a near miss, not necessarily a hit. The excellent data the U-2 provided was very valuable to us, but we could accept its eventual loss with the assurance that other means of gathering such information would become available.

To my knowledge, no one asked us what effect an incident involving the U-2 over Soviet territory on the eve of an Eisenhower-Khrushchev meeting would have. I have always assumed that the scheduling of the flight was routine. All such matters, like the cover story that came unglued, were *operational*. In the clandestine side of CIA, operational details were jealously guarded and made known only to those people directly involved on a strict need-to-know basis. We understood this thoroughly on the estimative side, made no effort to know, and felt no need to know. I must confess also that at that period of CIA's development there was a considerable "us-against-them" attitude. Most of us on the estimative side had little or no knowledge of the techniques of clandestine work and were prone to scoff at the excessively tight security about operations and to sneer at the bumbling of "the spooks." The clandestine people, on the other hand, disdained the academic attitudes of my side. They were doers, not contemplators, and they approached foreign affairs from precisely the opposite vantage point. Also, they could point to several loose-lipped indiscretions by one or more senior estimative people that they claimed had blown operations. So there was a wall between the two sides on all operational matters.

After Gary Powers's capture, for this reason, the reactions of the clandestine people and the estimative people were quite different. The operators reanalyzed the techniques and procedures surrounding the flight, especially the inadequately constructed and executed cover story. The analysts, in turn, concentrated on the impact the incident would have on Soviet behavior and the future of U.S.-Soviet relations. On one point we came close to agreement, although for different reasons: we both regretted President Eisenhower's forthright acceptance of responsibility for the overflight.

To the operators, the president's statement violated a basic principle of covert operations: plausible denial. All sovereign nations occasionally feel the need to undertake official actions that, for good and sound reasons, they wish to conceal from an adversary, either active or potential. In this instance it was the great need the United States felt to protect its security by knowing all it could about Soviet military power to strike us. When such operations are admitted by a nation's leadership, the operation is destroyed, and the success of other operations is placed in greater jeopardy. The better way is to deny the operation so long as that is plausible and then to place the blame on "excessive zeal" by the intelligence people. This, at least, preserves the decorum of international relationships, not a minor matter between superpowers. In Great Britain, very likely, the prime minister would have accepted the resignation of a minister or two and the incident declared closed. This is what Allen Dulles said one time in my presence should happen to him. "That's what I'm here for," he said with that easy Establishment manner.

The concern of the estimators regarding the president's admission was that it sharply curtailed Chairman Khrushchev's area of maneuver. Our feeling was that in great-power confrontations, like schoolyard arguments, it is better to leave a way out for your opponent unless you really want a full-fledged fight. With the wreckage of the downed U-2 and the captured pilot in hand, Khrushchev had essentially two options: he could accept some kind of apology and proceed to conduct Soviet policy toward the United States along its previous lines, including the planned summit meeting, or he could turn away, break off the summit meeting, and threaten other reprisals.

When President Eisenhower told him and the world that the U-2 flight over the Soviet Union was an official act by the United

States, one for which the president took responsibility, only the second of these options remained for Khrushchev. He could scarcely submit humbly, something no leader of a great power could do and retain his position. In light of these considerations, it seemed to us that Khrushchev had no choice but to break off the summit conference. After all, for one superpower to inform another (and the world as well) that it was violating its air space was at that time unprecedented. If Khrushchev's hand had been forced, so to speak, then the seriousness of his breaking off the summit meeting might be less than it seemed. Our assessment was that given the internal dynamics of the Soviet Union, including the faltering economy Khrushchev was determined to mend, he would try to squeeze every propaganda advantage out of the affair but not resort to much stronger measures at the time. We were about right.

The Bay of Pigs burst upon those CIA people not directly involved much as it did upon other Americans. To be sure, we knew something was afoot involving Cuban émigres if only by reading the *New York Times,* but we in the estimative side had not been informed about the CIA operation, nor had we been asked to make any judgment about the success of an American-organized landing. Our first reaction was to deplore the folly of this latest misadventure by "the spooks." Later, our view became slightly more sympathetic when we came better to understand the more limited objectives of the operation (Allen Dulles told me that the objective was not to precipitate a general Cuban uprising by a frontal invasion but to land a guerrilla force that could establish a base of resistance in the mountains) and when we realized how various restrictions placed upon the operation by the Kennedy administration had severely reduced its prospects for success. But we finally came to rest with the judgment that it was an ill-conceived mistake.

For young professionals in CIA who were to rise to leadership of the Agency in the 1960s, the Bay of Pigs was a watershed. This was true for emerging leaders in the clandestine services as well as those of us on the estimative side. The Bay of Pigs violated the first principle of covert action, plausible denial. First, it was too big; too many people not directly responsive to CIA discipline had to be involved; too much military materiel had to be assembled and maneuvered for it to be a plausible operation by Cuban dissidents; the hand of the United States was too visible in an attack only ninety miles off its shores. There may not be a precise size limitation for successful covert paramilitary operations, but the Bay of Pigs clearly exceeded any reasonable limit.

The dramatic and highly publicized failure and the subsequent ridicule and opprobrium that flooded over the Agency bit deep into us and created a new set of standards to apply to covert action. There was no comfort to be found in the knowledge that the Bay of Pigs had been a fully sanctioned U.S. government operation for which CIA was merely the executive agent. Whatever the responsibility for its inception, it had been a mistake. The Agency's capabilities had been misused. The disaster and its aftermath became an institutional memory, a guidepost, which lasted to my certain knowledge for at least the next ten years.

Back in the Fast Lane

8

The Bay of Pigs disaster swept a number of top men out of office, beginning with Allen Dulles, his deputy, General Cabell, and two other deputy directors, Richard Bissell, head of clandestine operations, and, indirectly, Robert Amory, head of reporting and analysis. To my considerable surprise it eventually touched me. This came about in a succession of events following the resignation of Bob Amory, who did not gain a new position in the shake-up and who felt that nine years as deputy director for intelligence was long enough.

The new director, John McCone, had been highly impressed with Ray Cline when he had met Cline in his post in Taipei. He requested Ray to come to Washington to take Amory's job as DDI, an offer Ray was only too happy to accept. Cline then asked me to leave the sedate life of a board member and take over a high-speed, high-tension job as chief of current intelligence. I likened it to asking me to step from a fur-lined bathtub out into the sleet and rain.

I, of course, declined. I had plenty of good reasons. First, why should I leave the job I had? A member of the Board of National

Estimates sat (as the briefers for the Office of Training said, fatuously, I thought) at "the pinnacle of CIA." Besides, no one had ever left the board unless he had reached retirement age or gone back to his university or law firm. It was unprecedented.

Moreover, viewed from the outside, the Office of Current Intelligence (OCI) looked to be a mess. The people Osborn Webb and I had rejected that day when we went up and down the halls looking for analysts for the new Office of National Estimates were now in senior positions in OCI. I thought of them as plodding, run-of-the-mill types. Also, morale in the office was said to be low. Straightening the place up and giving it a new sense of direction looked to be a formidable task.

Still, the idea had some appeal. I thought wistfully of getting back in the fast-paced daily tempo of current intelligence, setting my own standards, running my own show. I would be rejoining Osborn Webb who had been transferred to OCI six months earlier and knew the people. He would be my deputy once again. Finally, when I compared my present daily round of meetings, meetings, and more meetings with the prospect of publishing a daily intelligence newspaper against tight deadlines and responding to overseas crises with rush reports, I discerned the faint, leading edge of oncoming boredom. I told Ray Cline I would take the job.

Most of my preconceptions about OCI turned out to be wrong. The senior people we had left behind in 1950 were there all right, but just underneath was an office full of bright, highly educated, well-trained people. They were somewhat frustrated by a top-heavy system and the fuddy-duddiness of the people who ran it, but once a little light and air were provided by lifting off that top layer, they were eager and dedicated. One by one I moved the incumbents from their jobs as chiefs of the various geographic branches and replaced them with younger, more charged people. One or two of the older people left CIA; the rest I gave assignments as research analysts or support staff members. All this I was able to accomplish only with the inspired work of my administrative assistant, Robert Dixon. Most "admin" types use bureaucratic regulations as instruments of denial: "You can't do that!" Bob Dixon's approach was precisely the opposite: "Tell me what you want done, and I'll find a way to do it."

Then I overhauled the system for producing the daily publications and situation studies. I had found in place a phalanx of editors who constituted a gauntlet through which the analysts, the people who knew the score, had to run. The editors were simply that, not substantive minds but inserters of commas and revisers of phrases. I had learned by then that if an editor comes across a piece of prose, he is determined to edit it, no matter what. This phrase ought to come before that, this word is unnecessary, and so on. Lacking substantive background but having the power to make changes the editors often did violence to the judgments of the analysts, and even when that was prevented by impassioned argument they did substantial violence to analysts' sensibilities and pride. It was a bad arrangement. My solution was modeled after my early experience in ONE. The best work there had been done harmoniously when a senior man in the geographic branch had done the editing before bringing it forward for publication.

I broke up the phalanx and assigned a senior officer as editor to an individual branch, one for Western Europe, one for Near East, and so on. There he had to make his peace with the analysts daily, acquiring substantive background in the region by constant immersion. The adversarial relationship soon broke down, and the analysts learned that the editor of their branch was their best ally in getting pieces accepted by Osborn Webb and me for the publications.

The younger people I had found in OCI were a new breed, the second generation of CIA analysts. Unlike their predecessors who were often World War II stay-behinds or retreads, they were professionals by education and experience. Most of them had studied intensively the region to which they were assigned. For the most part, they had entered CIA directly after university. Many had advanced degrees, a number of master's and a few Ph.D.'s. One Near East expert periodically took leave of absence to teach his

147

subject at the Johns Hopkins School of Advanced International Studies. I once asked him when he was going to leave the Agency to teach full time. "Never," he said. "There simply isn't any other place in the world where I could be as well informed about the Near East. When I leave to teach I am astonished how far behind my academic colleagues are. I can't wait to get back and get caught up."

That was the lure that snared and held top-notch regional specialists in CIA. When an analyst arrived at his desk in the morning he found the major newspapers, a swatch of clips from the Associated Press and United Press International tickers, a batch of cables from the overnight take, and a handful of intercepted messages. In sum, he had on his desk each morning virtually all the information about his specialty that the United States had acquired in the previous twenty-four hours. The cables included highly sensitive messages from ambassadors to the secretary of state, routine analyses by foreign service political officers, observations by U.S. military attachés, and espionage reports from CIA operatives. For the student of foreign affairs it was a cornucopia.

On most mornings, an analyst's first task was to sift through this material in search of a significant new development, headline stuff, suitable for one of the daily publications. When he found one, he whacked out a rough draft and turned it over to his branch editor. Then he sorted through the rest, looking both for material to put in his background files and information suitable for a think piece about emergent problems that could someday erupt into crises. We called such a study a "CIA memorandum." As a series, they were distinguished, insightful pieces of scholarly journalism, far deeper in draught than anything in *TIME* or *Newsweek*, and laced with secret information not available to journalists. John McCone, who succeeded Allen Dulles as director of CIA in 1961, was quickly impressed by the quality of the work coming out of OCI. He said to me one day, "You ought to call your place something else. You do so much more than current intelligence." We searched for a more descriptive name for the office but found none we liked.

Anyway, our bread-and-butter operation was the daily publication, the successor to Harry Truman's newspaper. But it was true—we did so much more.

In 1961 the lineal descendant of President Truman's newspaper was thriving, having matured into an all-source publication of authoritative depth and scope. It also had a most distinguished offspring, designed by Huntington Sheldon and Richard Lehman, in direct response to President John F. Kennedy's request. We called it the *President's Intelligence Check List.* This was a no-holds-barred publication that carried CIA operational reports and other information too sensitive to be placed in the *Current Intelligence Bulletin.* Our best writers, led by Dick Lehman who writes with a warm, direct, somewhat Thoreau-like style, produced a brief, elegant account of the morning's intelligence news. President Kennedy wanted it on his desk at 8:30 A.M. To meet that demand, our writers arrived in the Langley headquarters at 5:30, and the editor, Osborn Webb or I, came in at 7. Shortly after 8 the *Check List* was handcarried to the White House by a senior OCI officer who stood by to answer questions the president might have.

There were only half a dozen top officials on the distribution list. (Stewart Alsop in *The Center* referred to me as "the publisher of the most expensive newspaper with the smallest subscription list in the world.") President Kennedy liked the *Check List* and entered enthusiastically into an exchange of comments with its producers, sometimes praising an account, sometimes criticizing a comment, once objecting to the word "boondocks" as not an accepted word. For current intelligence people, this was heaven on earth! A president who read your material thoughtfully and told you what he liked and did not like! Unprecedented then, unique still.

Here was another of the lures that bound our analysts to their work, to know that the *Check List* (later, at my suggestion, retitled the *President's Daily Brief*) would put your judgments before the president, to know that even in the standard publications your views might guide the secretary of state or defense. Whatever you wrote, you knew that your analysis of foreign affairs would appear under the authoritative seal of CIA and be distributed to the top policy makers of the United States. Unfortunately, you had to recognize that your region was not always on the front page. Months might pass while events plodded along without any hint of upcoming problems. This kept the analysts searching and probing so that once again they could be the center of the Agency's attention, their reporting and analysis being rushed to the White House. I once explained this to John McCone who had suddenly become concerned that because he and the White House had their attention riveted on Cuba, other parts of the world were being ignored. "Every analyst," I said, "wants his country to be the banner headline of the day. Down in OCI right now they are all eagerly scanning the day's take for that scrap of intelligence that signals a crisis for them."

John McCone as director of CIA lifted the Agency's estimating and reporting a full quantum jump in quality. He did it by devoting high seriousness to the work, demanding our very best effort, accepting only excellence and precision. To some of us, his keen intelligence and his balanced, objective viewpoint came as a surprise. What we knew of him in advance was that he was a very wealthy businessman, a dedicated Republican, and a devout Catholic with a reputation as an intense anticommunist. None of these attributes promised freedom from bias. We were ready to batten down the hatches and weather a stormy passage. My first encounter with McCone came shortly after his arrival while I was still making the transition from Estimates to OCI. We were presenting him with our just-completed estimate on Soviet advanced weaponry, seeking his approval before presenting it to the U.S. Intelligence Board. In Allen Dulles's time I had waited with six or eight other officers long hours in his anteroom to discuss our latest estimate, only to find that he had not read it and had only the faintest interest in it.

Our reception by John McCone could not have stood in greater contrast. At four o'clock precisely, he walked into the director's conference room with our estimate in his hand. "I have read your paper," he said, "and I have just three points I want to discuss." These three points proved to be the key judgments we had made about the state of the Soviet economy, our view that the Soviet leaders would be guided by caution rather than reckless adventurism, and the numbers we had estimated for one new weapons system. These three points were the very heart of the Soviet estimate. McCone did not oppose them out of hand, but he wanted to be convinced that we had solid data and supporting arguments to buttress our judgment. The discussion was thorough and searching, but after thirty minutes or so the new director pronounced himself satisfied. At no time had he shown any discernible bias. What he brought to bear was a judicious skepticism. We left the session relieved and delighted.

I came to know the quality of John McCone's mind intimately over the ensuing four years. Deputy Director (Intelligence) Ray Cline persuaded Mr. McCone to start his daily director's staff meeting with a current intelligence briefing. As chief of current intelligence, the job fell to me. I found it an intense experience. When I briefed John McCone he looked directly at me with his attention focused like a laser beam. Or, to use another simile, he plugged into the briefing like a five-pronged power tube in a high-fidelity amplifier. Nothing got by him. Now and then I would look up from my notes as he barked out a sharp question and realize that he was inexplicably angry. It invariably developed that I had just said something that was contrary to a view he had expressed in some other setting, perhaps a congressional hearing and possibly a year or two previously. Organized like a meticulous file cabinet, his mind could produce everything he knew, precisely and instantly. Before a new entry could be made, his mind had to be satisfied that it accorded with material already filed or that adjustments were feasible and proper.

In his professional role, John McCone was exacting and direct to the point of brusqueness. He tolerated no shilly-shally or dawdling. When he ordered something there was a steely-eyed glance that conveyed "right now and do it right!" This was so characteristic that Sherman Kent used to delight in asking senior CIA officers, "What color are John McCone's eyes?" The answer was always some variant of "ice-cold blue." They were in fact dark brown. But it was true, his mind and persona were steely-blue eyed.

Only once did I feel the steel. One morning I was reporting to him some new data we had just received about a Soviet strategic weapon and some preliminary judgment as to its significance. He interrupted me. "You know, I heard that same report in the Pentagon yesterday afternoon, and they drew the directly opposite conclusion."

Undismayed, I said, "Well, Mr. McCone, with the information we have so far it is easily possible for two people to look at it and arrive at contrary conclusions."

In white heat, he said, "You know damned well that isn't so. Your people are just sitting on their behinds and not doing their job!"

I was so surprised, so taken aback by this unjust accusation, that I fired back without thinking, "I don't agree with you for an instant, Mr. McCone, and I will be glad to discuss this with you on some other occasion!"

There was a hushed silence in the room while my fellow officers and I waited for his response. He glared at me for what seemed a long time and then looked away. He became all bonhomie and smiles as he went from officer to officer asking if they had anything they wished to bring up. The invitation I offered was never taken up; he never boarded me with pistol drawn again. The next morning he greeted me kindly, "Well, Jack, how is your world today?"

Running the Office of Current Intelligence turned out to be great fun. In the early 1960s some new international problem was always emerging that needed flash reporting and quick analysis. We ran a twenty-four-hour-a-day shop. The CIA Watch Office, into which cables and reports poured day and night—as I once observed, it is always noon somewhere in the world, and someone wants to tell you about it—was under my jurisdiction. I had a telephone at my bedside with a direct line to the CIA switchboard. When I left my home in the evening my first act was to provide the Watch Office with a telephone number where I could be reached. The watch officers were given specific instructions about when the director and the rest of the CIA command should be alerted, but when they were in doubt they called me to make the decision. Whether it was a coup in Iraq, an assassination in South America, an incident at the Berlin Gate, or the gunning down of Robert F. Kennedy, the decision had to be made at two, three, four in the morning as to whether to wake the director and the rest of official Washington. It was part of the job.

It was also a seven-day-a-week job. We published the daily periodicals on Saturday, and it was assumed that OCI would be staffed for emergencies for the better part of the day. Sundays I either went in to the office to read the overnight take or had a swatch of priority cables brought to my house by a security officer. Day and night the CIA parking lot is always well-stocked with cars.

During my four-year tour in OCI the world rumbled and shook to such crises overseas as rioting in the Panama Canal Zone, the Tonkin Gulf incident, the Chinese communist detonation of a nuclear device, and the dispatch of U.S. forces to the Dominican Republic. But the development that involved us most intensely was the Cuban missile crisis.

Early in 1962 we began to observe and monitor unusual shipments by the USSR into Cuba. Based on secret reports and previous experience, our analysts were able to determine that military materiel was in the holds of most of the ships. Soon we began to get reports that Soviet missiles were arriving in Cuba. This magnified the threat tremendously, and the Kennedy White House told the world that the United States would not tolerate the introduction of offensive weapons capable of striking the United States. Up till then, we had evidence that the USSR was sending antiaircraft, surface-to-air defensive missiles but no indication that surface-to-surface offensive missiles were arriving. The eye-witness reports of huge missiles moving down Cuban roads at night were not decisive because they were the reports of untrained observers, often peeking out the edge of window blinds, who could not tell the difference between a shrouded 35-foot-long defensive weapon and an offensive one. To a layman, the Soviet SA-2 looks big enough to destroy half the eastern seaboard of the United States.

Nonetheless, everything suggested that the Soviet Union was mounting a large military supply effort in Cuba, the purpose of which was anything but clear. We formed a twenty-four-hour Cuban task force in OCI and scrutinized every report thoroughly for clues. Meanwhile, the large Cuban exile community in the United States began to beat the drum. The press and several politicians, most notably Senator Kenneth Keating of New York, took it up. The heat on us was intense. We certainly had no reluctance to discover and report the presence of Soviet offensive missiles, but we could not find decisive evidence. Report after report turned out to be demonstrably false, the work of Cuban exiles who hoped for a U.S. intervention in Cuba, or uselessly ambiguous. Overhead photography revealed a widespread cloud cover throughout most of the summer but no Soviet offensive missile sites.

What we did find, through a variety of means, was a large surface-to-air network in the making. The size of this deployment did not in itself seem significant. The Soviet antiaircraft SA-2 is apparently one of their great engineering and manufacturing successes. When they get such a success they seem to open the spigot and let it run almost without regard to need or military requirements. Throughout the 1950s we had watched them splash SA-2s all over the Soviet Union, often in greater number and in places for which U.S. military men could find no reasonable justification. The Soviets also had bestowed SA-2s lavishly on their Eastern European satellite states. So, to us it seemed neither particularly surprising nor significant that SA-2s were going into Cuba by the boatload. What better way to instill confidence among Cubans against the looming U.S. threat?

To Director John McCone, this was not persuasive. He was confident that investing so many SA-2s in Cuba meant that the Soviets intended to deploy something they wished to protect: offensive missiles to threaten the United States. When the Office of National Estimates put out an estimate in September saying that placing offensive missiles just off our front porch would represent an extreme, uncharacteristic gamble by the Kremlin and therefore was unlikely, John McCone fired off a cable from his honeymoon retreat in the south of France. He disagreed. Events, of course, proved him right, though possibly for the wrong reason, and the official CIA estimate wrong although the way the crisis finally played out suggests that the CIA reasoning was not wholly incorrect.

Our uncertainty about Soviet intentions in Cuba abruptly ended the afternoon of 15 October 1962 when the first U-2 photographs came in. They clearly portrayed the characteristic deployment pattern for Soviet medium-range ballistic missiles. The only remaining questions were: (1) How many would they deploy? (2) How soon could they be operational? (3) Were nuclear warheads in Cuba for the missiles? We set the analysts to work probing for answers. We also mounted a round-the-clock situation report team, with a special publication to be ready each morning for the high-level policy team the White House had gathered to deal with the crisis.

By Saturday evening, the president and his advisers had made the decision to impose a quarantine around Cuba. They also produced a phased program for implementing it. The president was to make an announcement at 7 o'clock Monday, 22 October. Heads of state for close allies of the United States were to be briefed on our discovery of the Soviet missiles an hour or so before President Kennedy's speech so that they might listen sympathetically to his proposed plan of action. Senior CIA officers were to present the briefings.

The CIA Watch Office tracked me down Saturday evening shortly after I had arrived at a friend's house for dinner. In my office in OCI I found Ray Cline and Osborn Webb. The plan, Cline said, was to fly briefers to Europe and the various capitals the next morning. Sherman Kent, an excellent French speaker, would go to Paris to brief President de Gaulle; Chester Cooper, who had been stationed in London, to brief Prime Minister MacMillan; and I to brief Chancellor Adenauer in Bonn. The immediate task was to select the photographs and prepare the briefing, which was to be made up in several sets. Osborn Webb and I sat down at a large table with several experts and got to work. When we had it blocked out, I went home to get some rest and pack.

The next morning we three CIA officers arrived at Andrews Air Force Base. To our surprise we found that former secretary of state, Dean Acheson, and Ambassador Walter Dowling were going to fly with us on the plush White House Boeing 707. Acheson explained that he was going because Ambassador-designate Charles Bohlen was "on the high seas en route to France." Dowling, the U.S. ambassador to Germany, was returning to his post from consultation in the State Department.

Shortly after we were airborne, Dean Acheson strolled back to where the three of us were inspecting the briefing packages. "Have you something to tell us?" he asked.

I explained that we ourselves were seeing the completed briefing for the first time but would shortly have something to tell them. A little later I gave the briefing to them in the form the three heads of state would hear it. Acheson said he was satisfied and invited us to join him for a predinner martini. Sherman Kent asked in somewhat shocked tones, "Do you drink liquor on government airplanes?" "When you travel with me you do," said Acheson with royal simplicity. Throughout dinner he regaled us with a steady flow of urbane, sophisticated conversation. He also told us that during the week-long meetings he had held out for "a surgical strike," but the decision had gone to a quarantine. His tone of voice suggested some skepticism about the effectiveness of the action.

We put down in England at a U.S. Air Force base where we were met by U.S. ambassador to England David Bruce carrying a pistol in his overcoat pocket. "I got this mysterious message," he said. "I didn't know what to expect." Having dropped off Chet Cooper we flew on to the military section of Orly Air Terminal in France. There we dropped off Acheson and Kent. When Dowling and I disembarked at Köln we were met at planeside by Brewster Morris, my National War College classmate, then deputy chief of mission at Bonn. He took me off to his lovely residence on the banks of the Rhine where the hooting of tugs and barges woke me at six o'clock the next morning.

Ambassador Dowling and I set off for our appointment with Chancellor Konrad Adenauer Monday about 6:30 P.M. All day long apprehension had been growing in me. First, as to the encounter with Adenauer himself, I had been warned that he might be highly skeptical and a tough nut to crack. But far more important, I was concerned about what events might flow from President Kennedy's challenge to the Soviets. Having gone so far and taken the risks of putting offensive missiles under our noses, would they submit quietly and withdraw them at our request?

We found Chancellor Adenauer relaxed and jovial. When Ambassador Dowling introduced me, the chancellor, then in his early eighties, looked skeptically at me, ancient eyes crinkling in his weathered face. "Are you sure your name is Smith?" he asked. "Perhaps you have *zwei Name.*" Uncertain whether this was just another quip about the ubiquity of the name, Smith, or an allusion to the practice in the German secret service of invariably using a pseudonym in professional situations, I replied simply that my name was indeed Smith. He then invited us to join him in a snack of coffee and little sandwiches. The three of us sat on a long sofa before a large mahogany coffee table. After a few minutes of chatting, I called for the armed courier to bring in the briefing materials. He entered, carrying the large valise containing the blown-up U-2 photographs mounted on boards approximately three feet by four feet. The chancellor looked at the enormous carrying case and then asked me gravely, "Do you sleep in there at night?"

The briefing went smoothly. Far from being skeptical, Adenauer said he was not really surprised by the Soviet action, seeming to imply he believed them capable of any devious maneuver. He ventured to display a little technical background by asking whether the Soviet missiles pictured on their launchers were "cold" or "hot," that is, cryogenic or noncryogenic. After fifteen minutes or so of informal discussion, the remarkably sharp, clear pictures resting among the coffee cups at knee level directly under the old man's eyes, he turned to the ambassador and said, "You may tell your president that I will support him in meeting this challenge." Mission accomplished.

After dinner that night with Brewster and Ellen Morris, we listened to President Kennedy's speech (midnight, Bonn time) disclosing to the world what American intelligence had discovered in Cuba. We looked solemnly at one another and wondered, "What next?" What was next for me, I decided, was to get back to Washington as quickly as possible. If war was to come, I wanted to be back at my job and with my family. I was aboard a Lufthansa flight from Köln at eleven o'clock the next morning and arrived in New York barely fifty-four hours after I had left. A CIA security man approached me at the New York airport gate. "Mr. Cline is here in New York at the UN, and I'm to take you there to join him." I sure as hell did not want to stay in New York, so I went instead to the nearest telephone booth. Ray, it turned out, was assisting UN Ambassador Adlai Stevenson by providing him with the latest intelligence and, judging by his voice, having the time of his life. He wanted me to assist him and share the excitement. I argued that I could be more useful to him back in headquarters by making certain he got what he needed. I also urged that one of us ought to be back running the store.

The next day I was back at my OCI desk scanning the incoming messages about the Soviet ships that were then in mid-Atlantic, heading south and approaching President Kennedy's quarantine line. The tension grew. The United States and the Soviet Union were head to head, eyeball to eyeball. Then word came that a Soviet ship had stopped; it was dead in the water. After what seemed an interminable wait, the ship turned about and began the long voyage home. As Secretary of State Dean Rusk said in memorable phrase, "The other fellow just blinked."

In succeeding weeks we inspected innumerable pictures, taken by Navy aircraft a bare fifty feet above the sea, of Soviet ships leaving Cuba with the controversial missiles on their decks. The Soviets had brought them into Cuba tucked away in the hold, but to facilitate our inspection they loaded them out on deck for the trip home. Moreover, the Soviet crews obligingly pulled back the protective shrouds covering the weapons so that we could make an accurate count. To me, the pictures of those Soviet seamen, faces peering up at the U.S. Navy plane roaring overhead while they held the shrouds aside, formed an incredible, vivid portrayal of surrender. Kennedy had outfaced Khrushchev. The Soviet gamble had failed.

A few weeks later a call came from the White House for my services. It seemed Chancellor Adenauer was coming to Washington on a previously planned visit, and it was felt desirable to give him a briefing on the resolution of the Cuban missile crisis. "You convinced Adenauer that the missiles were there," said McGeorge Bundy. "It's up to you now to convince him they are gone."

On the appointed day I arrived at Mac Bundy's office, accompanied by a courier and the enormous valise. "Where is the briefing to be?" I asked.

"In the cabinet room."

I went up the back stairway and down the hall to the cabinet room. It was empty because the German party and their American hosts were all out in the Rose Garden, just beyond the glass doors, going through some kind of military honor guard ceremony. I had assumed that Chancellor Adenauer and I would be closeted in some small anteroom with his interpreter for the briefing. Instead, I found the cabinet room set up in full ceremonial panoply, the Germans deployed on one side, the Americans on the other, with President Kennedy and the chancellor facing each other in the middle of the long table. At the end of the room, a good thirty feet away, stood the easel on which I was expected to place my pictures.

I went back down to Bundy's office. "I can't brief that old man like that," I said. "His old eyes could never find the missiles in the pictures. I'm going to put the pictures down right in front of him. That's the way I briefed him in Bonn."

"Do it any way you like," said Bundy. "It's your show."

Back upstairs I pushed a few things around and made space for the large boards directly in front of Adenauer's place. Then I sat down behind his chair and waited. The party came in the doors opposite me, President Kennedy handsome, affable, and breezy. "Now we are going to give you a briefing on the removal of the Soviet missiles from Cuba," he said. "At least that's what we think we're going to show you. Of course," he said airily, "we don't know for sure whether they were ever there at all." Broad, winning smile. "All right," he said crisply while gesturing toward the easel at the end of the room.

I stood up behind Chancellor Adenauer. "Mr. President, I thought I would put the pictures down in front of the chancellor."

"Let's get on with the briefing," he said imperiously, again gesturing toward the far-away easel.

I tried again. "I believe the chancellor can see the pictures better here." This time Bundy intervened on my behalf, and the president said, "All right, start the briefing."

I leaned over Chancellor Adenauer's shoulder as I placed the first board down before him. "Chancellor Adenauer, I am Mr. Smith."

"*Immer!*" he said, instantly and dryly. The translator said, "Still!"

I was so taken by surprise that I burst out laughing and then looked up to see President Kennedy, Dean Rusk, and Robert McNamara all staring at me. I tried in a few words to explain the joke: "When I was in Bonn the chancellor had difficulty believing my name was really Smith."

160

Back in the Fast Lane

"Let's have the briefing," said the president unsmilingly.

So I launched into a ten-minute accounting of the exodus from Cuba of the Soviet medium-range missiles. At one point a well-tailored arm reached over my shoulder and pointed at a shadow in one of the pictures. "That's one of our planes," said that unforgettable Boston-edged voice. It was the only time I was ever assisted in a briefing by a president of the United States.

At other times in my career I briefed other heads of state (I believe my final score was four presidents, six prime ministers, and a like number of foreign and defense ministers), and I had a few other accomplishments of which I am reasonably proud, but I am certain that for many of my colleagues the peak of my career was established in Chancellor Adenauer's joking disbelief that my name could really be Smith. For a time I was known alternatively as "Immer Smith."

To put the Cuban missile crisis to rest, I think American intelligence, and especially CIA, experienced one of its finest hours. Despite intense political and media pressure, we held steady and acted responsibly and with integrity. We did not succumb to a temptation to accept as valid the flood of refugee rumors and reports—the "where there's smoke, there's fire" syndrome—but we sifted and sorted until we finally got the evidence that enabled us to target the U-2 correctly. Derided as incompetent by the likes of Senator Keating, we did not panic or bail out. To have acted with any less responsibility and integrity would have been a keen disservice to the president and the country. Like President Kennedy, we met the challenge.

After the tumult of the Cuban missile crisis we went back to the standard flow of international events, an Iraqi coup here, a Soviet provocation there, a governmental collapse there. Each day I briefed John McCone about the shape of "my world," as he called it. One morning in this period remains vivid in my mind. The evening news the night before was shrill in warning of an oncoming heavy snowstorm. Around eight o'clock snow began to fall in gusts and waves. Eight to ten inches were forecast. One

161

or two inches paralyzes Washington, but eight to ten inches promised collapse. How was I to get to work next morning from my place tucked into the rolling hillsides near Great Falls? After dinner I put on rubber boots, gathered up a snow shovel and a large broom, and drove my twelve-year-old Plymouth up the nearby steep hill and parked it in a churchyard. From there I had a reasonable chance of getting out to the main roads in the morning.

In the black predawn I climbed out of bed and started a pot of coffee. By six I was slogging through a good ten inches of fluffy snow up the steep hill to my car a third of a mile away. With the broom I got enough snow off the car for visibility; with the shovel I cleared enough track to get started. The ancient engine started cheerfully, and I set off on my way. I was the first man out, and with a virgin, unrutted road to deal with, I made it down to Langley with no great difficulty but with a considerable sense of achievement. With the New York Times, the Washington Post, and a full-sized helping of overnight cables under my belt, I was primed and ready for John McCone when he entered the director's conference room on the stroke of nine. While we waited for the others to get settled, I looked down at my feet and noticed my shoes were dusty from being worn inside boots. My eyes glanced over at Mr. McCone's feet and noted that his shoes sparkled and shone like new patent leather. Stepping out of his house onto a soliticiously cleared walkway and into a carefully prewarmed limousine that drove into the Agency's heated garage and stopped fifteen feet from his private elevator, Mr. McCone had experienced none of nature's harshness. "You know," I said to myself, "that SOB doesn't even know it snowed last night."

The year 1963 moved along pretty routinely until November brought the unthinkable tragedy of President Kennedy's assassination. I was at lunch in the grill room of the Fort McNair Officers' Club when the bartender hushed the room with the shocking announcement that the president had been shot and was en route to a hospital in Dallas. I telephoned the CIA Operations Center

162

immediately; they had nothing to add. I ran out to my car and drove out the George Washington Parkway with all the speed the old Plymouth could muster. Having no radio I was in darkness, and I vowed never again to own a car without a radio. By the time I reached the Operations Center the end had come. Later that afternoon I went down to the director's office with a roundup of worldwide reaction and activity, especially Soviet. Mr. McCone, I learned, was spending the afternoon at the nearby Robert Kennedy home consoling the president's brother.

The next day I accompanied John McCone as he went down to the White House to brief President Lyndon Johnson. We found the newly installed president in the basement secretarial offices. He came out of McGeorge Bundy's office and stood amid the clutter of secretaries typing and telephones ringing and talked briefly with McCone and me. Beside the compact, trim McCone he looked massive, rumpled, and worried. He had no interest whatever in being briefed, and after some inconsequential chatting, he turned back into Bundy's office. We had no way of knowing it, but we had just witnessed a preview of McCone's future relationship with Lyndon Johnson.

John McCone stayed on as DCI under President Johnson for another eighteen months, but it became clearer and clearer to us who worked with McCone closely that it was not a satisfactory situation for him. The president's chief intelligence officer must have ready access to the president if he is to carry out his mission effectively. Moreover, it must be comfortable access. Both men must feel easy, confident of the other's support. All DCIs want exactly this, but its achievement is more often desired than realized. It cannot be legislated or commanded. It is the product of personal chemistry and compatibility of mind. It even comes down to the personal preference of the president for the mode by which he receives information: orally or in writing. Richard Helms, who later established an almost ideal DCI-presidential relationship with Lyndon Johnson, says that Johnson much preferred reading to listening—short memorandums over spoken briefings. McCone's crisp, concise sentences, spoken in his usual brisk manner, fell on deaf Johnsonian ears.

Rumors began to float through CIA halls that McCone might soon be returning to California. Inevitably speculation about his successor became a favorite sport. Everyone selected a favorite candidate. Many distinguished Americans were named as potential choices from outside the Agency, but among officers within CIA the speculation circled around just three: Richard Helms, head of clandestine services; Lyman Kirkpatrick, executive director; and Ray Cline, DDI. Surprise was total, and for two CIA candidates chagrin was evident, when the announcement came that Admiral William Raborn was to be our new director. At his daily morning meeting, Mr. McCone let it be known, his voice and expression conveying displeasure, that he had not been consulted.

The Raborn Episode

9

The swearing-in ceremony of Admiral William Raborn was a typical Lyndon Johnson show. The White House made it known it wanted a large CIA delegation present, so all the office and staff chiefs were summoned to attend. We clustered in little knots awaiting the president's arrival. One exception, I noted, was James Angleton, chief of counterintelligence, easily our most clandestine member. Jim took his position alone in the farthest corner. Soon, Lyndon Johnson surged into the room like the incoming tide at the Bay of Fundy. He shook hands ceremoniously with about half the guests and then summoned Admiral Raborn to stand beside him in the farthest corner, a spot that commanded the entire room but also ensured that Angleton would be prominently pictured in every photograph taken during the swearing in. His anguish was visible.

President Johnson informed us that he had confronted an exceedingly difficult replacement problem with the departure of John McCone, but he had met the crisis by searching the country from one end to the other for just the right man. Finally, he had found him: "Red" Raborn. The president went on to say a few more words, which all presidents feel obliged to say, about the sensitivity and high significance of CIA work and declared his full confidence in Raborn's patriotism and his ability to carry out this great task.

I had known Admiral Raborn slightly during my service with the NSC staff in the Pentagon. He was at that time just concluding his highly successful and widely celebrated management of the Polaris program. He completed the project fourteen months ahead of schedule, an almost unprecedented feat. *TIME* magazine placed his cheerful red face on its cover. Upon his retirement, one of the giant aerospace corporations in California made him a vice president with a generous salary and representational allowance. Raborn, a rabid golfer, bought a house beside a fairway on a posh course at Palm Springs and settled down to enjoy the fruits of his success. It was from this that Lyndon Johnson had plucked him, working apparently from the mysterious assumption that demonstrated skill as a naval program director would qualify him to direct the arcane, sophisticated enterprise that CIA had become by 1965.

When I shook hands with Admiral Raborn immediately after President Johnson's little speech, tears were coursing down his crimson cheeks and forming tiny drops at the point of his chin. Raborn was above all else an unabashed patriot; at the president's request he would have gone to Patagonia. Knowing his history and realizing the enormity of his forthcoming task, my heart went out to him. "We'll make it work, Admiral," I said when I congratulated him on his appointment.

The point need not be belabored. Admiral Raborn's background did not qualify him to direct CIA. He had no extensive service overseas; he knew little about foreign affairs and had little interest in international politics. He knew no more about intelligence methods and techniques than the average naval officer. He believed himself to be a competent program manager, and that is where he eventually made a useful contribution to CIA. But before then there were a number of rough moments that caused maximum frustration for CIA career officers and for the admiral himself. The saving grace

166

during this period was that Lyndon Johnson had named Richard Helms as Raborn's deputy director. Dick's cool, experienced hand kept the good ship CIA from careening onto the shoals on more than one occasion.

Raborn had barely got seated in the director's chair when Lyndon Johnson decided to intervene with U.S. forces in the Dominican Republic. Civil war had broken out, and the Castro-supported side seemed likely to win. This put CIA in its crisis mode, which involves speeding intelligence-collection operations, moving information swiftly to the White House, the State Department, and the Pentagon, and producing hourly situation reports for policy people. Admiral Raborn, with only a novice's understanding of how internal CIA mechanisms meshed but having great confidence in his skill as an expediter, decided he could contribute best by locating precisely where in the CIA building incoming messages were received and rushing them directly down to the White House. Dick Helms's smooth intervention prevented the disaster that is risked when raw, unevaluated intelligence reports are placed in a president's hand.

But Admiral Raborn's energy and his strong drives did result in one organizational improvement that has served the Agency well ever since. For several months, Ray Cline and I had discussed setting up in the Office of Current Intelligence an operations center through which *all* incoming intelligence would be funneled, thus providing a central point for the director and his deputies to look for the latest information, especially during crises. At the time of the Dominican crisis we already had a DDI Watch Office, the lineal descendant of the group I had established during the Korean War in 1950. But this fell short of being a CIA operations center because CIA clandestine reports came in directly to the deputy director of plans (DDP), where a separate twenty-four-hour watch group was set up during crises like the Bay of Pigs. The importance of CIA clandestine reporting for following and understanding the Dominican affair highlighted the necessity for having everything CIA knew in one place. With Admiral Raborn's energetic support and Dick

Helms's blessing, Cline and I set up a CIA crisis task force in the operations center that merged DDI and DDP elements together. It was the first concrete expression of a new relationship between the clandestine services and the research and reporting side of the Agency, a relationship that expanded and bloomed later under Dick Helms's leadership.

The Dominican Republic crisis soon passed into obscurity with the establishment of a new government under President Balaguer. Our attention swung back to Vietnam. The year 1965 turned out to be a watershed year in Vietnam, it being the year President Johnson decided to up the military ante with sizeable infusions of new American forces. "Nailing the coonskin to the wall," the president's graphic and extravagantly optimistic phrase, was the expressed goal. Sanction for proceeding at flank speed was given by Congress in the Tonkin Gulf Resolution, a congressional response to an obscure and controversial incident involving U.S. Navy destroyers.

On a dark night in the Tonkin Gulf off North Vietnam two U.S. Navy destroyers reported they were under attack, their sonars indicating incoming torpedoes. Although they were never able to sight their attackers, it was assumed that North Vietnamese torpedo boats had launched the reported torpedoes. Neither destroyer received any hits, and eventually the apparent attacks broke off.

From the outset, CIA military analysts were skeptical of the actuality of the attack. Sonars on fast-moving destroyers are subject to numerous anomalies, such as large fish or schools of fish, temperature inversions, and even the sound of nearby friendly ships. A ship's propellor chops holes in the water, so to speak, an action termed "cavitation." There was a suspicion that the destroyer sonars were picking up their own and their companion's cavitation. Our judgment on whether Vietnamese boats had attacked U.S. destroyers was suspended. The evidence we had did not establish or refute the fact.

To my surprise the White House decided, without consulting CIA, that the attack was a reality and that it justified expanding the U.S. war effort. Much of the White House case was based on a report that indicated such an attack was planned. We, of course, had seen the report but had discounted it heavily because we had found the source previously unreliable. To CIA, it proved nothing. Mystified, I telephoned a White House aide who had been involved in handling the incident in the White House situation room. Incidentally, this man had been a National War College classmate. "We got this report from the State Department," he said, "and when we checked back, they seemed to think it was authentic."

"But why in hell didn't you call us about it?" I asked. "We're the authority on such stuff." His lame excuse was that there was not enough time. The president was passing orders virtually directly to the young commander on the destroyer's bridge and wanted confirmation immediately.

Later on, the feeling became fairly widespread in Congress and the press that Lyndon Johnson had all but fabricated the incident and had used it to con Congress into giving him wide latitude in fighting the war. My own guess is that confusion prevailed, both on the destroyers in the Tonkin Gulf and in the Oval Office. A strong predisposition to believe the worst, combined with an inadequate understanding of the quality of intelligence the White House was dealing with, did the rest. A blunder but not a baleful blunder. It goes without saying, of course, that Lyndon Johnson was quick to perceive the leverage the attack gave him, real or not.

One day Ray Cline called me into his office. Door closed, he told me he wanted to make me his assistant deputy director so that I could take over the DDI while he was traveling or taking leave. Since he already had three assistant deputies, one for special intelligence handling, one for administration, and one for liaison with policy people in the NSC, this took some explaining. Knowing Cline's soft-hearted reluctance to offend a subordinate in any way and suspecting that he did not want to wound two of the three by naming one of them as superior to the others, I tried to decline. He did not need another assistant deputy. Besides, if he did want one I was not the man for it. "We're too much alike, too easy and kind," I told him. "What you need is someone who can be a real son of a bitch."

"Jack," he replied with a soft smile, "I think you underrate yourself." Aside from dealing a severe body blow to my self-image as a scholarly, gentle type, his answer seemed to leave me no riposte. And no choice but to accept. As it happened, Cline's absence for extended periods in the months to come gave me the opportunity, as acting deputy director, to work more closely with Dick Helms than I had before.

It was apparent that Ray Cline was restive under Admiral Raborn's directorship. Cline and John McCone had enjoyed a close and fruitful working relationship. Each appreciated the intellectuality of the other, and Cline reveled in the priority McCone accorded DDI work, as opposed to the dominance of the DDP under Allen Dulles. Cline had the very highest regard for John McCone and found the contrast to his successor painful. He was not alone. Stories began to circulate in the Georgetown cocktail circuit about Admiral Raborn's shortcomings, especially his lack of knowledge of foreign affairs. Some suspected that Cline was the prime source of such stories, something I sincerely doubt. In any event, the atmosphere grew increasingly uncongenial to Cline, and he asked finally that he be reassigned, preferably overseas. Dick Helms arranged to post him to Germany.

Shortly before the announcement was made, Helms told me that he and Admiral Raborn felt I was Cline's logical successor. Did I want the job? I had already thought about it carefully and answered yes. While acting as DDI I had observed several places in the organization where I felt changes should be made, both in personnel and structure. I looked forward to trying my hand. Dick Helms, a convinced "don't fix it if it works" administrator, looked at me skeptically. "Don't make any big changes without checking with me first." I agreed and became deputy director for intelligence in January 1966.

As DDI I had charge of all the CIA intelligence analysis, research, and publication intended for outside dissemination. In

170

essence, the DDI is the voice of CIA on foreign political, economic, and military affairs. The exception, of course, was the national intelligence estimates, which were historically intended to be intra-agency, *national*, and reflect the judgment of *all* the U.S. foreign intelligence agencies—the State Department, the Defense Intelligence Agency (combining Army, Navy, Air Force, Marine intelligence), and the National Security Agency. Over the years, the original concept of joint estimates had been severely eroded by the greatly enhanced scope, depth, and sophistication of CIA analytic work, with which the other agencies had failed to keep pace or had even retrogressed from their 1947 stature. To a greater extent than many wished to recognize, the estimates had become substantially a CIA product, dependent almost entirely on DDI political and economic analysis. My predecessor, Ray Cline, felt that this consideration, added to the long-standing traditions that the DDI was the chief substantive officer of the Agency and ONE was organizationally subordinate, made him responsible for final review of the estimates. My old chief, Sherman Kent, resisted with his usual energy and formidable invective.

When I became DDI I made it clear to both Kent and Dick Helms that I had no such aspirations. Despite the realities, it seemed to me highly valuable to the director of central intelligence to maintain the traditional concept of joint estimating that was expressed within the Agency by making separate the Office of National Estimates and the DDI, the Agency's voice. It was valuable to the DCI in his relationships with the other intelligence chiefs and the secretaries of state and defense whose support he often required in overseas operations. It also gave him the backing he sometimes needed when making controversial judgments stick with the White House. Besides, it looked to me as though the DDI had more than enough under his control without reaching for more.

In 1966 the DDI had seven main components and several staffs. Of the seven, four were analytic facilities: Current Intelligence, Economic Research (formerly "Research and Reports," which I renamed to match its mission), Basic and Geographic Intelligence (which I combined from two entities), and the National Photographic

171

Interpretation Center (operated by CIA through the DDI as a joint effort with the Pentagon). Two components were overt collection facilities: Contacts, with offices nationwide to tap the voluntary assistance of U.S. scientists, academics, and corporation technicians; and the Foreign Broadcast Information Service, a worldwide organization for recording public radio broadcasts with intelligence utility. The seventh was Central Reference, which stored and retrieved intelligence materials and operated the CIA library.

After combining one or two offices with closely related functions and replacing one or two office chiefs with younger, more highly charged officers as I had done when taking over OCI, again with the "can-do" help of Mr. Fix-it, Bob Dixon, my first priority as DDI was to pull together the several groups in the Agency who were working on military intelligence. The effort was dispersed and piecemeal. I picked Bruce Clarke, Jr., a sharp, aggressive man, to study the feasibility and advantages of combining the separate groups into a single office, and on the strength of his report, I created the Office of Strategic Research under Clarke's leadership.

This was considered a bold stroke. By long-standing custom and, for a time, mutual consent, military affairs was held to be the exclusive province of the armed services. Military intelligence was thought to be too specialized, too arcane for mere civilians, a view revived in the late 1970s by General Daniel O. Graham without notable success. Unfortunately for that concept, the military services throughout the 1950s and 1960s had consistently displayed an inability to make objective, dispassionate judgments regarding the strategic threat, with the Air Force leading the rest in flagrant disregard for impartial assessment. For reasons easy to perceive, military intelligence analysts invariably leaned toward the worst case, the maximum conceivable threat. From my two years' service in the Pentagon and five years on the Board of National Estimates I knew that the president and the National Security Council were ill served by such work. It was time for CIA to assume the role in military affairs it already had attained in international political and economic realms. The Office of Strategic Research constituted

172

a statement to other intelligence agencies that CIA had a professional competence in strategic military affairs. Under Clarke it soon
became a strong voice in the field.

Besides its somewhat loose-jointed structure when I took over,
the DDI was in practice a set of separate duchies, especially in
producing intelligence reports. The economic analysts set about
writing their studies with little or no consultation with the political
specialists in OCI, who responded in kind. Consequently, studies
on a country of current significance emerged separately from the
two offices sometimes a week or a month apart. Not only was
such timing poor service for our readers, but each study could have
been enriched by merger with the other. I felt the DDI needed to
take a more active part in pulling together the effort of his
directorate. The answer was to set up a publications board with
regular meetings.

The publications board also exercised control over DDI resources. DDI analysts had always responded like fire horses to the
alarm to any request for a study; the motto was "If someone asks,
we'll do it." It was a custom established in our early, scrambling
days when we hungered for attention and recognition. As a result
I found analysts tied up for weeks on an exhaustive project of
value only to a low-level specialist in the State Department. When
asked why, either of two stock answers was given: "If we don't
do it, no one will"; or "If we don't do it, someone else will do it
badly." Both possessed a certain logic but provided an unsound
basis for structuring the work of a strategic analytic group. At
the new publications board, requests were reviewed and approved
or rejected. Rejection was so alien an idea that I used to ask the
office chiefs to join me in saying no: "All together, 'No'!"

The other administrative procedure I changed was the selection
of officers for choice appointments. We had a dozen or more places
where we could send people for beneficial experience, including the
National War College and three or four other armed services schools,
the State Department Senior Seminar, and a handful of overseas
posts. They were all admirably suited to broaden an officer's

experience and expand his horizons as I well knew from my National War College year and my Singapore tour. The difficulty I saw was that the most qualified were not always selected. Much of the blame rested with the office chiefs who understandably wished above all to hold on to their most talented and productive people. When they were asked for a candidate they often offered someone they could well spare or someone who was troublesome, a "problem child." To deal with this, I first asked the office chiefs to give me a list of subordinates they expected to rise near the top. We called it a "Comer's List." Then I stipulated that only people on that list were eligible for these choice appointments, and only those on the list were eligible for promotion to the higher grades. I also insisted that a higher ranking job be waiting for an officer returning from one of these choice appointments. He could not go and return to his old place. These new arrangements made for some very lively discussions with the office chiefs, but as a result we got better qualified representatives and CIA benefited.

With these administrative changes put in action, I felt the DDI decks were cleared for better operation. As an aside, the most surprising find I made during the process, which extended over several months, was that I actually enjoyed it, a startling discovery for someone inclined to think of himself as a reflective, studious type. I also enjoyed being the DDI despite its fifty- to sixty-hour demand. The amount of daily reading was prodigious: two newspapers, thirty to forty selected incoming cables, the output of the four intelligence publication offices, including final review of the *President's Daily Brief* before publication, a half-dozen administrative memorandums, and odds and ends of State Department and Pentagon publications. I usually arrived in my office about eight and prepared myself for the director's morning meeting at nine.

I had risen at six, breakfasted, and read the *Washington Post* before leaving the house. At my desk, I found the *New York Times*, a sheaf of priority cables, and the morning CIA publications. These had been pulled together by my admirably thorough executive assistant, Karl Wagner, and neatly arranged by my excellent and authentically beautiful secretary, Yvonne Daughtry. In the next hour I decided which item of news I wanted to discuss at the director's meeting and which DDI study I wished to summarize. The morning intelligence briefing would be made by Drexel Godfrey, my choice for successor at OCI who had come to us from Williams College and was a recognized scholar of French governmental affairs. At nine I was ready.

The director's morning meeting was an admirable institution in CIA. At nine each morning the director assembled in his conference room his top command, approximately ten to twelve officers. First came a seven- to ten-minute worldwide intelligence briefing, then each officer was given an opportunity to speak briefly about any matters of general Agency concern within his purview. Examples might be a disagreement with other intelligence agencies, congressional concern over an overseas crisis, forthcoming visits by American or foreign dignitaries, a breakthrough in handling some vexing operational or administrative problem, and so on. The director described conversations the day before with the president, secretaries of state or defense, or congressional leaders. By 9:25 or 9:30 we were back at our respective desks. Rarely did a meeting last as long as forty minutes. But during that brief time the CIA leadership had established a common understanding of where we were and where we were headed. The director had issued his instructions without the exchange of memorandums. The only record was that of the executive director, Col. Lawrence K. White, who kept brief minutes and sent one-sentence action memorandums as reminders to the appropriate officers. Outside management experts admired this institution for its efficiency.

Admiral Raborn retained the custom and presided over the morning meeting with his usual good cheer and optimism. Occasionally, he would growl at us to "get off our diddy-boxes" and get on with the job. Such impatience usually was passing, though. He tried hard to get to know us all during his brief tenure and systematically invited two or three of us at a time with our wives to informal dinners at his home. Admiral Raborn soon realized that

175

his most effective contribution could be made in the area of resource management. An age of austerity was dawning for the first time in CIA's history, and the recognition was growing that the Agency needed to improve the way it allocated resources. Raborn's impetus was most timely, therefore, and by the time he left, an Agency-wide resource management system was an ongoing concern.

I cannot leave Admiral Raborn without telling one story involving him and John McCone. Mr. McCone had business interests in New York that required him after his retirement to come east from California several times a year. He always took the occasion to come to Washington, and when he did the Agency provided him the services customary for a former director: a limousine, an intelligence briefing, and any other assistance we could reasonably give him. In the first year of his retirement from CIA, McCone made two or three such visits. Invariably he called on Admiral Raborn and offered his unsolicited advice on a wide variety of matters, concentrating on how the current DCI should handle things. When word came on one occasion that McCone was coming our way, Admiral Raborn called me in to tell me he did not want to see McCone, and I was to handle the problem. Now Admiral Raborn was as eager as the next man to have his inadequacies in the job meticulously pointed out to him by his predecessor, but the fact was that he was suffering from a horrible cold and wanted to see no one. He was sitting at his desk with a large Kleenex under his nose to catch the steady drip when he gave me my instructions.

At Dulles airport I met McCone with two limousines, one for his wife and one for him so that I could give him the customary intelligence briefing on the way into his hotel. I informed him, as instructed, that neither the admiral nor his deputy, Dick Helms, was at headquarters so we would drive him directly to his downtown Washington hotel. Without comment, McCone said to the driver of Mrs. McCone's car, "Take her into the building at Langley." As I followed him into our limousine, I said, "Oh, you want to go into the building? Then we can finish up our briefing in the anteroom just off the basement garage." But when we arrived in the anteroom,

Mr. McCone seated his wife on one of the sofas and said to her, "I'm going upstairs for a few minutes." As we rose to the seventh floor on the director's private elevator I said, "We can go to my office, Mr. McCone, for our discussion." But as we got off the elevator, I turned right in the direction of the DDI's office while he turned left toward the director's suite. I wheeled around and followed. McCone sailed into the director's outer office at flank speed and without breaking stride opened Admiral Raborn's closed door and walked through. The admiral sat at his desk, a miserable figure still clutching a piece of Kleenex. Before he even sat down, McCone had already said, "Admiral, there are a couple of things I want to take up with you." I stood behind him silently indicating my helplessness. As I retreated in chagrin I met Dick Helms coming in the doorway, and my defeat was complete. As I explained to both men later, I could not have stopped John McCone from confronting Admiral Raborn that day except by a hard tackle below the knees. The admiral smiled weakly and said, "I know. You did your best."

Admiral Raborn went back to his aerospace corporation in June 1966 without tears and, so far as I know, without regret. He left behind some personal friends in CIA who admired his patriotic acceptance of the task the president had forced on him and respected his dogged cheerfulness in trying to carry it out.

The Golden Helms Years

10

Smiles lighted faces in the gray halls of Langley in 1966 when Richard Helms's appointment as director became known. His appointment signified recognition of CIA's mature professionalism. One of our own, a man from the ranks, had been chosen to lead us. The clandestine services were especially pleased because they had felt neglected under John McCone and uneasy under Admiral Raborn. Dick Helms they knew as a sure-footed, cool professional, the very model of a new breed in American government service, the professional intelligence officer.

Some skepticism tinged the smiles of the estimators and the analysts. Although they did not know Dick Helms firsthand, they knew his experience had been entirely in espionage, and they feared he would neglect analysis in favor of clandestine operations just as Allen Dulles had done. My own feelings were entirely positive because I had come to know Helms through a link to our mutual past, Williams College. One morning during the Cuban missile crisis while waiting for Director McCone to arrive, Helms approached me and pointed with pride to the leading article in the Phi Beta

Kappa *Key Reporter,* which he said was written by his old professor. The author was Hallett D. Smith, a scholar of Elizabethan literature at Williams College. Hallett, it seemed, was Helms's favorite professor, while Helms was Smith's "best student." Hallett Smith was also one of my closest friends at Williams; it was in his living room that I had heard the fateful news about Pearl Harbor. The insights into the mind and values of Dick Helms that I acquired through this relationship gave me considerable confidence that his leadership would be broad-gauged and liberal-minded. I was not disappointed.

Helms's leadership enabled CIA to become a unified, cohesive organization for the first time in its history. As DCI, meeting regularly with President Johnson, secretaries Rusk and McNamara, and JCS chairman Earl Wheeler, Dick Helms saw very clearly the high importance of the CIA publications, the work of the DDI analysts and the ONE estimators. He was now held responsible for their shortcomings, their inaccuracies or vagueness owing to inadequate reports from overseas, and he also was credited with their successes, applauded when they were on the mark. His control of the clandestine services and his unique prestige among the operational people gave him the leverage necessary to make clandestine effort more responsive to the needs of the analysts' needs, which, Helms now fully perceived, were direct reflections of needs of the president and his principal lieutenants.

In the past, rivalry and suspicion had dominated the relationship between operators and analysts because, as I have mentioned, of the operators' concern over lax security in handling their hard-won secret reports and the analysts' scorn of the seemingly exaggerated secrecy of the operators. Ray Cline, a former clandestine officer himself, had made a beginning in bridging this gap. Now, under Helms's urging, the two sides of the Agency began to deal more freely with one another and to understand the other's needs and difficulties. Simultaneously, the atmosphere of freer exchange and unified effort, which Dick Helms gave fresh impetus each day at his morning meeting, embraced the two other main components

180

of CIA, Science and Technology under Carl Duckett and Support under Robert Bannerman. Confidence in each other replaced rivalry and suspicion. We felt we were joined together in running a strong, capable organization, one able to respond quickly and skillfully, to get things done without bureaucratic formality and delay. We took great pride in those qualities that set us apart from old-line government agencies: direct, common-sense answers instead of bureaucratic jargon; quick response to requests—minutes and hours instead of days and weeks; can-do instead of delay and evasion. The year 1966 opened a golden era in CIA's history.

A few days after my appointment as DDI, Desmond FitzGerald, then deputy director of plans, stopped me as we were leaving the morning meeting. "How about having lunch with me Friday?"

"Love to. Anything special in mind?"

"No. Just general discussion of anything you want to bring up. Ray Cline and I started having weekly luncheons a few months back, and we found them useful in ironing out little problems between our two directorates."

"Great. It's a fine idea." But as I walked back to my office I wondered what might really lie behind Des FitzGerald's invitation. Des was a delightful, intriguing man with the silken grace and easy manners of a courtier and the imagination and dash of a Renaissance soldier of fortune. I often thought that Des would have been in his element in the Elizabethan or Stuart eras of sixteenth or seventeenth century in England.

My previous encounters with him had left me a tad wary. Once, when I was writing a national estimate on the Philippines, he appeared at my desk, debonair in a Panama straw hat, offering to provide me with any and all clandestine reports his Far East Division possessed on the Philippines. Since this was unprecedented and unique, I quickly realized that Des was guided by motives other than cooperation for its own sake, perhaps some operational gain he perceived in getting the Philippine story more fully told.

On another occasion, at a morning meeting, Des presented a report from a Far East chief of station, a man known for his

181

unreined imagination, wild-eyed to the point of irresponsibility at times. This report suggested that the Chinese communists might as a propaganda maneuver transport a nuclear device to Indonesia and permit their Indonesian communist clients to detonate it, thus causing a wave of fear to sweep through Southeast Asia and bringing greater prestige to Indonesian communists. I thought it was preposterous and launched into a speech of several minutes detailing what made it unlikely that the security-minded Chinese communists would risk letting their highly prized nuclear technology leave China for, of all places, Indonesia. When I had finished, Des smiled his most charming smile and said, "What Jack has said is exceedingly logical. But this is not a logical situation. It's *psychological!*" A man as slippery as that needs watching, so I wondered what might lie in store at the Friday luncheon.

My wariness was groundless. In the private dining room near his office, FitzGerald began by asking whether my people had any specific problems or complaints regarding clandestine reporting. I had come armed with one or two that I passed along. He took notes and promised a response by Monday. He then said that his people were sometimes puzzled by their inability to get some of their best reports into the high-level daily publications. We agreed to set up a meeting between his top reports officer and the editor of the daily bulletin. And so it went. Dealing directly, not through subordinates or through Helms, we sorted out many vexing problems between the operators and the analysts and thereby improved the performance of both. How much improvement was graphically demonstrated a couple of years later when we did an analysis of the contribution made by clandestine reporting to the top-level daily publication. We were astonished to find that nearly *one-third* of the items over a month's time could not have been published in the absence of a key clandestine report. Since most of us had always assumed that such reports represented at most about 10 percent of published intelligence, this was amazing. It was also a tribute to the cooperation of Desmond FitzGerald and the leadership of Richard Helms.

Just such leadership was called for in 1966. The Vietnam War had become a major American undertaking requiring massive support from all the national security agencies, the Middle East was a volcano about to erupt, and the Soviet Union appeared to be approaching a new frontier in advanced weaponry. But above all, the Vietnam War absorbed our attention and our energies. Under Lyndon Johnson, Vietnam was literally a twenty-four-hour-a-day preoccupation. The president was fired by his ambition to nail the coonskin to the wall.

The perception of the Vietnam War within CIA was considerably less positive. Despite the president's intensity and surges of oceanic energy, the U.S. war-making programs in Vietnam were not making decisive impact. It fell to CIA, as the objective monitor of overseas developments, to pass this unwelcome news to the White House. One such uncongenial message was a study we titled "The Will to Persist." The U.S. objective in Vietnam was to make Hanoi request a negotiated peace, a request the government was not going to make so long as it had "the will to persist." The CIA study sought to assess the strength and well-being of the North Vietnamese will to fight on and to make a judgment about its life expectancy under American attack. Our study, based on a detailed analysis of the elements of North Vietnamese strength, came to the pessimistic conclusion that U.S. programs, both under way and planned, were not likely to break the enemy's will in the foreseeable future.

We did not expect congratulations from the White House. Instead, I thought I might get a telephone call from Walt Rostow, the presidential assistant for national security affairs, as I had in the past, asking me to rework our data some way or another to see whether a different result might emerge. To our surprise, President Johnson told Dick Helms he found "The Will to Persist" a first-rate job and asked that he present it to several top leaders in the Senate. The wily Lyndon may have seen in the study support for his determination to press the war more strenuously, but in any event we found encouraging his willingness to accept bad news. We had more in store. One Saturday morning when I was acting DDI in Ray Cline's absence, Defense Secretary Robert McNamara paid us a call. He had with him Cyrus Vance, his deputy, and John McNaughton, his assistant for international political affairs. I was amused to note that Vance and McNaughton both spoke in the exact staccato style of McNamara and seemed to vie to get off their own machine-gun bursts in the brief intervals between McNamara's. The secretary wanted us to analyze the success of the U.S. Air Force bombing program, code-named "Rolling Thunder," specifically how successful it was in blocking the shipping of materiel south into the battle zone. We had first-class competence in Vietnam logistics in a team headed by Paul Walsh, an economist from the Fletcher School of Tufts University, but still this was an unusual request for a secretary of defense to make of a civilian agency. I assumed that McNamara was asking us to work with the Pentagon on the project, but to make certain, I asked him whether he wanted us to coordinate our work with the Defense Intelligence Agency. "Certainly not," he barked. "I know what the Air Force thinks; I want to know what your smart people think."

With this charge to conduct an independent study, we set to work. In two weeks we produced an intensive logistic analysis that demonstrated Rolling Thunder was not significantly slowing the flow into South Vietnam. Although American Air Force bombers were hitting depots, highways, bridges, and trucks, the North Vietnamese were moving their shipments in small lots down the wooded mountain paths known as the Ho Chi Minh Trail. An important component of the CIA study, difficult for the American military to accept, was that logistic requirements for the Viet Cong and North Vietnamese field units were extremely small, especially as compared to U.S. Army needs. Not only did they use their ammunition more frugally, but their food requirements were minimal. Moreover, they did not haul in Coca-Cola machines, movie projectors, and other accoutrements of American civilization. They could meet their needs by strapping 150-pound bundles aboard bicycles or bicycle-wheeled carts and pushing them up and down the mountain trails, their movement invisible under the heavy canopy of leaves.

Our pessimistic finding could not have brought joy to Robert McNamara's heart, but he was nonetheless impressed with the quality of our analysis and requested that we repeat a Rolling Thunder assessment on a quarterly basis. The successor studies continued to demonstrate unflinchingly that Rolling Thunder was failing in its objective. We finally determined that the North Vietnamese in the teeth of the U.S. bombing program had improved their capability for moving war materiel south *fivefold*. Secretary McNamara continued to praise CIA work, and one morning at his nine o'clock meeting Dick Helms reported that in a conversation at the White House the day before McNamara had spoken of the "magnificent support" CIA was providing him.

Which brings me to a baffling aspect of Robert McNamara. All things considered, I would have said that McNamara made the most intelligent use of CIA skills and resources of any high officer I have ever known. He asked the right questions to get searching, insightful answers. He respected our analysis and our objectivity even when most uncongenial to his own goals and undertakings. On most occasions before departing on one of his many trips to view the war in Vietnam firsthand he asked us for an update on our assessments of the situation. Armed with these he would set out, and several days later, either just before boarding his plane in Saigon or somewhere en route, he would vent another of those incredibly optimistic statements about "light at the end of the tunnel." Perhaps, as secretary of defense he felt obliged to wave the flag and cheer the troops, but I never was able to determine whether his views had been really changed by the professional cheerleaders in the Military Command in Vietnam (MACV) or whether he was stifling his better judgment in the interests of morale.

McNamara was one top officer who appeared to be receptive of our judgments and to seek them out. Dean Rusk was a steady, low-key supporter of the Vietnam War, and although he did not take issue with our views, he also did not seem influenced by them. Walt Rostow, Lyndon Johnson's ebullient assistant, was a different matter. Rostow was a dynamic optimist and found our pessimism hard to accept. Many times he would question a CIA study and suggest that if our data were subjected to "rolling averages" or even more arcane statistical techniques the results would be more favorable. Rostow even took our data on occasion and reworked it himself, a procedure that horrified CIA analysts because they knew that intelligence data in the hands of amateurs is dangerous. Unlike economic and statistical data derived from hard fact, intelligence materials are based on reports of varying levels of certainty and reliability. Some reports will bear no more than the weight of a wispy guess; others can support an army tank or a national policy. Only someone who works with these materials every day has the knowledge to see this clearly and use the data wisely.

But what Walt Rostow did that horrified the analysts most intensely began on another occasion with a telephone call to me. President Johnson, Walt said, was making a speech in a few days and wanted from us a list of U.S. gains and accomplishments in recent weeks in Vietnam. I accepted the task and passed it along to the Vietnam team. I was not prepared for the reaction I got. In itself the request was unusual only in that it was for the specific use of the president. We were constantly being asked by senators and congressmen for such material and even on occasion for a completely written speech. I recognized that what was requested was one-sided, only the upbeat aspects of Vietnam, but our balanced judgments were clearly on record and were being reiterated daily. If the president wished to be optimistic in the face of our contrary view that was certainly his prerogative. I saw no problem in complying with the request.

But the analysts saw it differently. Within fifteen minutes a deputation of six Vietnam specialists was outside my door. Their message was they refused to do the job. The Vietnam War was not going well for the United States, and they would not be a party to claiming it was. That would be dishonest. I looked at the set, affronted faces before me while I pondered my next move. Finally, I asked Molly Kreimer, an OCI Vietnam specialist, what she thought we *could* do to meet the White House request. Molly suggested that we present a balanced statement, a racking up of recent gains as well as setbacks. "Fine," I said. "Make two sets of lists, one positive and one negative." Appeased, they went back to their desks, and the paper arrived in my office in a couple of hours. I shipped it off to Rostow who, I suspect, snipped off the negative side and kept the positive. In any event, the honor and integrity of CIA analysts remained intact.

We never had any illusions that Lyndon Johnson was being persuaded of our view of the war. One episode in particular sticks in my memory. We had completed a study at White House request on the pros and cons of a new American initiative that involved a substantial increase in the war effort. If one based one's decision on the conclusions of our study the result was obvious: the gain was not worth the cost. Nevertheless, the president announced the next day that he intended to go ahead. Distinctly annoyed that an admirable piece of analysis, done under forced draft at White House request, was being ignored, I stomped into Director Helms's office. "How in the hell can the president make that decision in the face of our findings?" I asked.

Dick fixed me with a sulphurous look. "How do I know how he made up his mind? How does any president make decisions? Maybe Lynda Bird was in favor of it. Maybe one of his old friends urged him. Maybe it was something he read. Don't ask me to explain the workings of a president's mind."

I retreated in silence, trying to absorb a hard lesson. It is one every professional intelligence officer needs to keep constantly in mind. National policy is formed from a welter of considerations, many of them conflicting with another. The president, the secretary of state, or any other high-level policy officer is assaulted and

187

besieged by these considerations in the shape of reports, conversations, telephone calls, news tickers, and his own recollections of past mistakes and triumphs. Lyndon Johnson kept five news tickers running outside his office door, and when he found an item that jibed with a pet idea he tore it off and carried it around in his pocket to be read at the right moment in discussions. In this hurly-burly, this Niagara flow of paper and words, national intelligence is just one voice. Ideally, it is the coolest and most objective, but still it is one among many and presents only a part of the problem. Who knows, maybe Lynda Bird *did* remind her father of some previous occasion when everything worked out just dandy.

Even though we never won the president over to our view about Vietnam, I never had any doubt while Richard Helms was director that we were reaching Johnson daily on other matters and possessed his confidence. We had won Johnson's confidence through one of our genuine intelligence successes, calling the shot on the Arab-Israeli Six-Day War.

For some months in 1967 it had been clear that tensions were building toward an inevitable clash between Arab and Israeli forces. Early in the year Drexel Godfrey, chief of OCI, suggested that to monitor this crisis a task force be established under the chairmanship of a doughty veteran Near East expert, Waldo Dubberstein. We made it a DDI-wide group with political, military, and economic specialists and charged it with making weekly judgments on the imminence of hostilities and the relative strengths of the opponents. One morning in May at the director's morning meeting I reported the most recent findings of the Dubberstein group: (1) war was imminent, and (2) the Israelis had the capability to win it in ten to fourteen days. Helms expressed immediate interest. "Are you sure of that?" He directed me to have the data thoroughly rechecked and report back to him. I did not know at the time that Dick Helms had just attended a White House breakfast at which the president had fretted about the pressure he was under from both the Israelis themselves and pro-Israeli members of his own government to increase military aid substantially to protect the Israelis from supposedly superior Arab forces. Our report could not have been more beautifully timed.

I did not learn until later that at this same time an Israeli paper making the claim they were badly outgunned by Arab forces had been passed to Sherman Kent, chairman of the Board of National Estimates, for review. The Dubberstein group's findings were reexamined, and the board put out a brief paper that refuted the judgment of the Israelis and supported the original position that their forces could prevail in ten to fourteen days. Helms sent copies to Dean Rusk, Robert McNamara, and Earl Wheeler, chairman of the Joint Chiefs of Staff.

President Johnson called a meeting of this group to decide whether further military aid should be rushed to Tel Aviv to meet the crisis the Israelis foresaw. As the group assembled before meeting with the president, Dean Rusk walked up to Helms with a curious smile. "Do you agree with this paper your fellows wrote?" Helms said he did. "Well," said Rusk, "all I can say to you is this: in the immortal words of New York Mayor Fiorella Laguardia, 'If this is a mistake, it's a *beaut!*' "

In the Oval Office Lyndon Johnson quickly read the short paper and looked over the top of his glasses. "Do you all think this is all right?" They all responded with nods and "ayes." Johnson turned to his military adviser. "You Wheeler?" When the general signified his agreement, the president ordered Wheeler and Helms to "scrub this thing down" and make certain it was correct. What emerged was a special national intelligence estimate that shortened the period the Israelis could be expected to defeat their foes from ten to fourteen days to seven to ten days.

There remained one key question: when would the war start? We were aware that among the Israeli delegation sent to Washington to pressure the United States for more arms was one key military leader, and we reasoned that if he departed suddenly the war would soon begin. When he disappeared overnight, a quick report was sent down to the White House, and several days later the 1967 Arab-Israeli War began and lasted, not seven to ten but, as we know, six days.

As Helms remarked later, it was "a tidy package." Best of all, it supported President Johnson's wish to ignore Israeli pressure and do nothing. He was extremely grateful to CIA and Richard Helms, and from that day forward Helms became part of the "Tuesday Luncheon" inner circle. This group, which also included Rusk, McNamara, and Wheeler, constituted President Johnson's personal council for dealing with international affairs. It did not always meet on Tuesday and not always at lunch, but it did comprise the men whose judgment Johnson most respected on foreign policy and military affairs. Helms rigorously avoided expressing views on policy, recognizing that to identify CIA with any line of policy would instantly dilute our credibility as an objective reporter, but he did speak up whenever one of the other members gave short shift to the facts in his zeal to press his case. "Mr. President," he would say, "we don't see it quite that way. Our reports suggest. . . ." This "keeping the game honest," as Helms called it, was highly valued by the president, and Johnson made it a point to keep Helms by his side, whether in Washington, Guam, or wherever.

This is the kind of direct access to the president's mind that every intelligence officer dreams about. To be certain that your reports reach the president's eyes and ears without the intervention of a phalanx of aides and assistants is the ultimate reward. It is seldom achieved, and Richard Helms's rapport with his president set a high mark in the history of presidential-Agency relationships. It served us very well throughout the Johnson administration and provided a cruel contrast to the subsequent Nixon years.

The CIA relationship with the White House was tested severely during a protracted and sometimes sharp dispute between CIA analysts and the U.S. military command in Vietnam (MACV) over the size of the enemy force. This same dispute erupted again much later, although in a highly distorted, simplistic form, in a 1984

CBS documentary program and a subsequent libel suit by General William Westmoreland against CBS. Contrary to the impression created by media coverage of the trial, the controversy was not a simple black-and-white affair in which one side lied ignobly and the other clung staunchly to established truth. It was instead a problem of high complexity where divergent views had valid claims to respectability. The sources of disagreement between the Washington civilian analysts and the Saigon military were many. They ranged from differing analysis of "spongy" evidence to opposing concepts of enemy force structure and even to the essential nature of the Vietnam War.

The storm center of the dispute was the number of irregular forces in South Vietnam, the guerrillas, the part-time saboteurs. The military worked with classical order of battle categories as taught at West Point, and their categories sometimes did not match the enemy structures confronting them. CIA analysts used more flexible concepts that seemed to them more consistent with Vietnamese organization. For example, in CIA tables a guerrilla was a black pajama-clad Vietnamese who might be a daytime shop clerk but who lent his services from time to time to blowing up a bridge or booby-trapping an abandoned hut. At MACV headquarters in Saigon a guerrilla was a member of a military unit subordinated to a village or district committee, a definition that inevitably produced a smaller number for the irregular forces than the looser CIA one. The dispute over the size of the irregular force was significant in its own right, but it reached hurricane strength when it was added to the number for main forces—over which there was little argument—and thereby produced a total for enemy forces in Vietnam far higher than MACV held.

To a degree, the sum produced by this addition was illegitimate. Vietnamese irregulars were saboteurs and sometimes assassins, but they did not have the same military value as regular forces. It was like adding pennies and dimes to silver dollars to determine how many coins you have and deducing from that number how rich you are. If you add enough pennies to double the total number of coins, are you twice as rich? That total figure, however, regardless of how it was achieved, had great potency for critics of the Vietnam War, both inside and outside government. As the Saigon military command foresaw, it could be—and was—used like a club by those opposing U.S. efforts in Vietnam.

The controversy lasted for months without resolution. Within CIA there was a gadfly, a junior analyst named Sam Adams, who devoted himself with passion and zealotry to the problem. Adams had done some intensive analysis of reports on the irregulars in a single Vietnam district. Sorting and sifting masses of low-grade reports, including notoriously unreliable captured-prisoner interrogation reports, he had emerged with a reasonably documented finding that the number of guerrillas in that district was considerably larger than the U.S. military figure and could possibly be double. This work was the seed that flowered in the CIA position that the figure for enemy irregulars should be higher than MACV believed it to be. The Saigon command would not accept that figure by itself, but when the number was added to the total force strength (illegitimately, they felt) and produced a doubling of the estimated enemy forces, they became adamant.

What was the proper role for CIA in this situation? Disagreeing with the military was no novel experience for us. We had been opposing U.S. Air Force inflated force projections for Soviet missiles and bombers for nearly two decades. But arguing about an estimated number of weapons not yet built and disagreeing with an American force in the field about the size of the enemy it actually faced were two different things. It was unprecedented for a civilian organization to refuse to accept the judgment of an army in the field where the "security of forces" principle prevails. But nonetheless the difference existed, born as I say of differing systems of reckoning, different interpretations of flimsy evidence, and unlike concepts of the nature of the war itself. Contrary to the suggestion in the CBS libel suit that Saigon suppressed the facts, all Washington knew about it. Congressional leaders asked anxious questions, the White House expressed its unease, Defense Secretary McNamara

192

wanted a resolution. No one put any pressure on us to knuckle under or to compromise. What pressure there was came from within ourselves. The president and the secretary of defense needed broad agreement about the size of the enemy fighting U.S. forces in Vietnam. If it was the task of any one in the U.S. government to establish that figure it was the task of the Central Intelligence Agency.

The zealots in our midst wanted us to rush into battle and carry the fight for Eternal Truth right up to the front steps of the White House. Calmer judgment among us recognized that our number, though arguably sounder than MACV's, did not represent eternal truth but was, like theirs, a series of compounded judgments and extrapolations. We recognized that in reality *there was no right number*. No one, not even the North Vietnamese themselves, knew exactly how many Viet Cong and related irregular units there were in South Vietnam. We were all feeling our way toward an approximation. Moreover, no matter how much passion we brought to the struggle, in the end the American leadership would be left with two different numbers. They needed *one*, one that represented the broadest possible agreement.

In summer of 1967, the issue came to a boil. We were preparing a national intelligence estimate on the situation in Vietnam, and the enterprise ran hard aground on the reefs that separated CIA and MACV. Seeking some way to extricate the estimate, Dick Helms sent his special assistant for Vietnamese affairs, George Carver, with several CIA experts out to Saigon. The ensuing discussions were hot and well-nigh bloody, but gradually it emerged that agreement could be found in three gradations: (1) substantial concurrence on main force (regular army) units; (2) rough agreement as to the approximate range of numbers within ancillary units (like 20,000 to 40,000); and (3) agreement that the difference over the irregulars responsive to military discipline was too great to allow quantification in a single number or a range. Accordingly, the three categories were expressed successively in single numbers, ranges of numbers, and words and phrases. The overall judgment of the estimate was that the size of organized opposition to the United States in Vietnam was on the order of a half-million.

We had done the best we could with an unprecedented and highly complex, recalcitrant problem. None of us was entirely satisfied with the result. We would have preferred to state without caveat the most defensible number our methodology could produce, but we recognized that to convince anyone else of the superiority of our number we would have to lead them step-by-step through the laborious, incremental series of judgments and extrapolations by which it was produced. No president or secretary of defense could be expected to do that. Our compromised position with MACV represented the broadest area of agreement achievable. It was therefore the most serviceable number for national planning, and we had the satisfaction of knowing that we had performed the task the Central Intelligence Agency had been created to perform.

Only a fraction of my ten-hour days as DDI were devoted to enemy troop numbers in Vietnam. A welter of other problems and decisions washed over my desk daily, but before turning to them one word more on CIA's role in steadfastly reporting hard truths about Vietnam. Sometime in the late winter of 1967 an initiative was offered for sizeably increasing, once again, the scale of the U.S. military effort. We were asked to do a study of similar efforts previously undertaken, and our findings were largely negative. At a subsequent White House meeting Secretary McNamara spoke up in opposition to the new proposal. "I have here in my hand," he said to President Johnson, "a CIA study that indicates such operations are not effective."

"But, Bob," said Lyndon Johnson, "you don't believe that crap, do you?"

"Yes, Mr. President, I do," said McNamara. This may have been one of the "last straws" that influenced Lyndon Johnson's decision not to run for reelection in 1968.

As I reflect on my daily activities as DDI I realize that some of them bore directly on two or three of the heresies that have gained credence over the past dozen years. One of these fallacious notions is that classic espionage, spies ferreting out secrets, has been superseded by high technology. This is the judgment of the half-educated. To give a contrary example, one time in the late 1960s we were collecting intelligence through technical devices, mostly photographs, that disclosed the construction of extremely large installations at several locations in a large communist country. We had seen nothing like it before, and we were perplexed. We called in outside experts who were as perplexed as we. A nuclear energy expert would proclaim, "I'll say one thing: it's *not* nuclear energy. Maybe it's poison gas manufacture." The poison gas expert would say, "It's *not* poison chemicals. Maybe it's nuclear." And so on. Meanwhile, we were wading around waist deep in technical reports, and nearly a year passed before we learned that the structures were munitions depots and strong points. If we had been able to position just one controlled agent on the architect's staff or the construction foreman's crew, the key to the puzzle would have been found and reported at once.

This is not to decry technical devices (audio devices, cameras, and the like) but to point out their limitations. They cannot look inside men's minds. They usually can tell you what is going on but seldom why. Moreover, they are grossly inefficient. They cannot be pointed as precisely as a human spy, and they spew out tons of irrelevant information that must be laboriously sifted to find the gold among the dross. The truth is that there is never enough *good* intelligence. We need all we can get of all kinds. Diplomatic reports, newspaper accounts, military reports, technical reports, espionage—they all form part of an intricate mosaic. Used with skill by an expert, they interact synergistically and establish approximate truth.

Another emergent heresy is that CIA analysts are influenced by academics and academic thinking to the detriment of realistic analysis. I am reminded of one venture we launched in the late 1960s to tap the knowledge and judgment of the best American scholars of Chinese affairs. Understanding what was going on inside China was a perennial problem for us, so when the DDI academic coordinator, John Kerry King, came to me with a proposal to seek outside help I was quick to approve. We set up three regional conferences, three days each, and invited the most prestigious scholars from the most prestigious universities on the East Coast, the Midwest, and the West Coast. Our experience at each conference was the same. The scholars were brilliantly knowledgeable of Chinese history, culture, and social structure, but they were as innocent as babes about current conditions, be they political, economic, or military. It invariably took the CIA Chinese experts at least a full day to bring the academic experts up to speed. After that, the discussions were useful but mostly corroborative rather than seminal. Incidentally, it was about this time that the Harvard Chinese scholar with the most famous name of all declared that "the most serious work on China is being done inside CIA."

I do not suggest that CIA Chinese experts were superior to established academic scholars. I do suggest that they were pursuing different activities with different purposes. For understanding the direction China is headed and the degree to which the United States would be either benefited or threatened by that direction, there is no substitute for examining analytically day-in and day-out *all* the intelligence the United States receives. Most CIA analysts found academic people too inadequately informed about current developments to have much impact on their judgment.

Perhaps the most remarkable heresy to emerge after Watergate is that prior to the Watergate great awakening, CIA was entirely without congressional scrutiny or control. This is nonsense. Throughout my entire career in CIA I participated in preparing a succession of directors for frank and open discussions with the designated congressional committees. I myself have spent whole days, three in succession, briefing congressional committees, passing along to them in closed sessions, our best intelligence on developments in nearly every country in the world. We answered their questions frankly and fully, sometimes writing detailed papers when the answer was not immediately in our heads. There was no holding back. When a new, potentially dangerous operation was about to be launched, the director usually briefed the chairman of our congressional committees privately and was then guided by him as to who else needed to be informed. Being frank and responsive with Congress was merely enlightened self-interest. We needed congressional support.

In pre-Watergate days Congress and CIA had a strong and effective relationship. We could brief Congress candidly, confident that our intelligence would not be leaked to the press and thus to the world and to our adversaries. At that time, Congress operated under the discipline of a strong committee system, the committees headed by men of discretion and integrity, giants like Senator Richard Russell of Georgia and Congressman George Mahon of Texas. The congressional leadership determined which committees or selected subcommittees we were to brief. We briefed only them. The leadership took responsibility on behalf of the rest of their colleagues for overseeing CIA operations. What has seldom been realized by the press and public about the heated demands for closer, more open congressional control of CIA is that to a fair extent this was a revolt within the ranks of Congress against the discipline of its leadership. Young Turks felt excluded by the Russells and the Mahons. They demanded, and got, participation by more of their number. Then, free of the former discipline, they felt free to leak to the press information about operations with which they personally disagreed. The result is the present chaos. When the *Washington Post* prints front-page stories describing congressional debate over whether to provide funds for CIA "covert operations," you know that the ultimate absurdity has been attained, an absurdity that entertains the civilized world and most notably the Soviets.

At this point, a word about the need for secrecy in intelligence operations. Gathering intelligence against a formidable opponent like the Soviet Union is a constantly shifting and evolving game of chess. We are constantly striving to find new ways to discern what is happening in their submarine construction pens or their nuclear-tipped-missile development facilities. They wish to deny us that knowledge. Sometimes the ability to get that intelligence requires months of high-technology work and the expenditure of millions of dollars—U.S. taxpayers' dollars. All of this flies out the window, becomes useless, as it did with the *Glomar Explorer*, when someone—a U.S. government official, a congressional staff assistant, or a congressman—decides that for some short-term advantage he will whisper a word in a reporter's ear or hand him a report. No one mentions, or seems to realize, the enormous waste of money and energy such leaks create. Maintaining official secrecy in an open society is admittedly a most difficult problem, one that raises fundamental concerns about democratic traditions. But no other open society in the world—and it behooves us to recognize that they do exist in England and Western Europe—finds it so intractable a problem as we.

As 1968 dawned and bloomed into full day I had a solid conviction that CIA had succeeded in securing its rightful position as the *central* intelligence organization of the United States. We were recognized as a source of objective and searching analyses of foreign situations. We were an essential part of U.S. strategic planning and operations. We were, in Stewart Alsop's phrase, at The Center. We stood at the elbow of the president, the secretary of state, and the secretary of defense. We could provide accurate background, hour-by-hour reporting during crises, long-range estimates, or even operational assistance.

In Vietnam, for instance, we were not only monitoring the progress of the fighting but we were heavily involved in the political side of the conflict. CIA's role in the so-called pacification programs, which were essentially efforts to beat the communist political action and terror squads at their own game, was central and enormous. We also invested large expenditures of effort and personnel in covert actions designed to help the military defeat the enemy. CIA's role as full-fledged partner in fighting the war in Vietnam was recognized and accepted in the White House, Foggy Bottom, and the Pentagon. That our participation in Vietnam should be so wholehearted, as contrasted with our pessimism about the progress actually being made, might surprise outside observers who view

CIA as a monolithic organization in which every analyst and agent marches in lock step. To us on the inside it was business as usual. Compartmented as we were, no obstacles or influences prevented analysts from calling the shots as they saw them. To the analysts, the CIA operators had no more claim on their favor than did the South Vietnamese army or MACV. Director Helms and his deputies, including me, made certain that it remained that way.

As the Lyndon Johnson presidency wound down in the election year of 1968 we faced the future with calm confidence. We were seasoned and established. We had made the adjustment from Truman to Eisenhower, from Eisenhower to Kennedy, and from Kennedy to Johnson. We knew what we had to offer and had every confidence that the new president, whether Humphrey or Nixon, would recognize its value. How wrong we were.

The Nixon Decline

11

The relationship between CIA and the Nixon administration began smoothly enough. About a week after the election the president-elect came to Washington to meet with President Johnson. At one point during the meetings the president called in Richard Helms, introduced him, and said, "I want Mr. Nixon to receive all the intelligence I am getting. Starting right away." When he got back from the White House, Dick Helms turned the problem over to me.

A slight complication was that the Nixon team had turned down the offices in Washington that Lyndon Johnson had made ready for its occupancy during the transition. The Nixon team had elected to stay in its campaign headquarters in New York, a labyrinthine maze of bedroom suites on the thirty-ninth floor of the Pierre Hotel. Richard Lehman, assistant director of current intelligence, joined me in the trip to New York to make arrangements. A severe snowstorm blanketed the East Coast that morning, grounding all air travel, and we journeyed north by train.

At the Pierre Hotel we were admitted to the presence of H. R. Haldeman, then as always wearing his hair in a 1940s collegiate brush cut. His manner was all matter-of-fact, unsmiling business. I explained what we needed: a twenty-four-hour-a-day secure room where we could house the teleprinters to receive the sensitive material from Washington and where a CIA officer could assemble the material and maintain the files. We wanted the space to be as near to the president-elect's office as possible. Haldeman shook his head. "Nothing here like that."

He pushed a buzzer and summoned a young man in his late twenties whose demeanor suggested a clerk in a men's clothing store. "Has the mimeograph room been cleared out over there yet?" The young man thought it had, so Haldeman turned back to us. "I can give you space in the basement of the American Bible Society building where we had our printing setup."

What Lehman and I found "over there" was a basement corner of a large office building, the floor and tables littered with mimeograph materials, the unfinished ceiling laced with electric cables and heating pipes. I was aghast, but a CIA security man checked carefully for electrical outlets and examined the flimsy door, which he said would be replaced and provided with a digital-release lock. "It will do," he said. During the ensuing week, security sent to New York two guarded trucks packed with sound-insulating materials, government-issue office furniture, and communications equipment. By week's end, in the basement of the American Bible Society building, looking precisely like dozens of offices in Washington, we had a secure room where we could safely receive and store the most sensitive intelligence materials.

The next step was to find a way to get these materials under the eyes of the president-elect at regular intervals. During the week we learned that Henry Kissinger was selected to be Nixon's assistant for national security affairs. I knew Kissinger slightly, having talked with him when he invited me to meet with his Harvard seminar that, unfortunately, circumstances later prevented me from attending. I telephoned him in Cambridge and made a date to meet him in New York immediately after the official announcement of his appointment. He arrived fresh from the press conference at the Pierre Hotel, seemingly a little surprised by his selection by Richard Nixon. "I don't know him very well," he said in his heavy, dark voice, the Germanic consonants hedging the vowels. "Talked with him briefly once at a cocktail party." Kissinger planned, however, on joining the Nixon entourage shortly and agreed that he could be the conduit for putting our publications and reports before Nixon.

Kissinger examined carefully the materials I presented, grunted approvingly now and then, but seemed puzzled by one aspect, the amount of reporting on Panama where there was at the time a fair amount of ferment. "Tell me," he said. "Do you have a regional quota for reports? So many for Africa, so many for South America?"

"No. Why?"

"I don't understand why you are paying so much attention to Panama."

I explained that in our view Panama was a potentially dangerous situation, dangerous to U.S. interests, and we wished to make the White House aware of it.

"But if anything happens there," said Kissinger, "I would simply turn it over to an assistant secretary of state. Our attention, the attention of Mr. Nixon and myself, is going to be centered on the Soviet Union and Western Europe." I did not argue, but I thought I knew from serving four previous administrations that pressures from Congress and the press would quickly cause changes in such a selective outlook. Subsequent history proved me right.

Before our interview ended, I made a strong plea to Kissinger to leave the interpretation of intelligence materials to us. "We will present it to you anyway you like; long reports, short reports, charts and graphs, or oral briefings. If you want us to refocus on a special aspect, just tell us. But please do not try to rework the materials yourself because intelligence evidence is tricky."

"Oh, no," said Kissinger. "You are the intelligence fellows. I will leave all that to you."

I left him feeling considerably more reassured than it turned out I should have.

Once established in the White House basement offices formerly occupied by McGeorge Bundy and Walt Rostow, Kissinger set to work establishing a formal, systematic structure for the preparation of national security policy papers. Essentially, he restored, amplified, and ramified the NSC structure of the Eisenhower days, a structure that had been neglected and all but abandoned by John Kennedy and Lyndon Johnson. He doubled, tripled, and quadrupled the White House NSC staff, siphoning off from CIA some of our most able analysts, including William Hyland, then a rising young Soviet expert, now editor of the prestigious *Foreign Affairs* quarterly. Several new subordinate bodies were created, among them the Senior Review Group, which gave a final review to policy papers before they were submitted to the National Security Council. Senior officers from State, Defense, and CIA formed the group; Dick Helms made me the CIA representative to attend the weekly meetings chaired by Kissinger.

It did not take long to realize that the reporting and estimating work of CIA would need extensive adjustment to meet the Kissinger-Nixon demands. Henry Kissinger's chief contribution to national policy planning was to establish a systematic array of options for each international problem in which the United States had an interest. Whereas in the past the State or Defense Department planners had examined the problem separately and determined which policy best met the situation, now they were required to produce several optional solutions, and CIA memorandums and estimates were needed to address each option individually.

Although the Kissinger approach has many theoretical benefits, in the real world there are some situations in which there are *not* several ways for the United States to deal with the matter. There may be only one, and other "options" are forced or artificial. I once watched a dramatic clash between the old and the new, the practical and the theoretical, when Malcolm Toon, later U.S. ambassador to the USSR, and Henry Kissinger argued heatedly over the necessity for options in dealing with a East European country. Kissinger could not believe there were no other options available, and Toon could not conceive of any realistic policy other than the one he offered. In the end, Kissinger had his way with the NSC paper in question, while Toon, banners flying proudly, stood his ground and won the battle in the real world of policy formation.

In CIA we did not feel we could ignore White House requirements to shape our work to fit specific needs, so we made haste to structure our papers along the Kissinger formalistic patterns. But not only CIA memorandums and estimates needed new formats. We soon realized that President Nixon was not reading the *President's Daily Brief* or, if he was reading it, did not like it. Because the publication was designed exclusively for the president and had as its readership only him and six other top officials, we felt it essential to deal with the matter. I made an appointment with Henry Kissinger and, when I arrived at his office, found with him John Mitchell, longtime Nixon crony and then attorney general. When Mitchell made signs of leaving, Kissinger urged him to stay. "You can advise us on this." I described our concern, and Kissinger said he had heard the president complain he could not distinguish fact from opinion in the *Daily Brief.* I explained that the easy style of the *Brief* had been designed to meet previous presidential requests but that we wanted to fashion it to President Nixon's taste. Did that mean he wanted no judgments from us, just a factual account?

At this John Mitchell rumbled into speech, his heavy dark voice brusk and his words so laconic as to seem grudging. "The president is a lawyer," he said as if this explained everything. "He likes to have the facts first and then the opinion."

That was all the guidance I could get from these two close advisers. On the strength of it we divided all *Daily Brief* items formally into sections of fact and comment. My impression is that it accomplished nothing and that Nixon continued to ignore our publication while relying on a daily compilation from Kissinger's staff.

Our first real clash with the Nixon administration came in connection with the annual national intelligence estimate on the

Soviet military force, specifically the capabilities of the latest Soviet ICBM, which we designated the SS-9, and its strategic implications. As DDI, I was not directly involved in preparing the estimate, but I received daily reports of fierce, ongoing battles between CIA and Pentagon representatives. Fights with the military, especially the Air Force, over the Soviet strategic threat were nothing new. We had been waging such battles since the 1950s. The brawling this time, as reported to me, sounded more ferocious, with the ONE people taking a line that began to verge on the intransigent.

Intelligence on the performance of the SS-9, still under development, was too sketchy to give either CIA or the Pentagon a solid base of fact. As in the case of the Vietnam numbers controversy, both extrapolation and speculation came strongly into play. The first point of dispute was the size and carrying capacity of the ICBM. The Air Force attributed to it gigantic size and enormous capacity; the CIA thought it was smaller. Next, came extreme Pentagon claims for accuracy of the new missile, an accuracy that CIA scientists said exceeded the inherent error in the geodetic grids then available. Then came the clincher. Both sides agreed the SS-9 was designed to carry a triple warhead, but the Pentagon claimed that each of the three warheads had a separate guidance system that took it to a designated target, and CIA held that the three warheads when released merely took a ballistic path like a bomb or a bullet. At this point it became clear, if it had not been so before, that the Pentagon was striving to establish the need for an American antiballistic missile (ABM) system. A large MIRV (multiple independent reentry vehicle) SS-9 would provide a threat great enough to justify an ABM, it was argued.

The battle now joined on the triple-warhead issue. When the CIA experts built too strong a case against the MIRV for the Air Force to withstand, the Pentagon made a tactical shift. If the three warheads were not separately guided, at least the Soviets could calculate with precision the pattern in which the free-falling warheads would strike, forming a "footprint." By plotting out these

206

footprints on U.S. Minute Man fields, the Soviets could be assured of knocking the force out before it could be launched. Secretary of Defense Melvin Laird, strongly partisan and highly combative, took the Pentagon interpretation to national TV and displayed with explicit charts before the country and the world just how these footprints would deal a deadly blow.

But the Pentagon experts knew the footprints rested on a slippery slope and found it hard to combat long-established principles of aerodynamics and ballistic trajectories that CIA brought to bear. The Pentagon people then moved on to a fanciful retargeting concept that caused Carl Duckett, CIA deputy director for science and technology, to label them "the inventors." The retargeting concept called for the Soviets to take a quick read of the SS-9's flight shortly after launch and to correct any error in flight that would cause a missile to miss its target. No one doubted that such a system could improve accuracy, but there was not a shred of evidence to support its existence, planned or actual, nor did the Soviets appear then to have the technology necessary to produce it. It was speculation of the purest cast, an invention.

These successive skirmishes eventually led to the final grand battle on the question: were the Soviets striving for a first-strike capability? Secretary Laird affirmed they were, saying that the powerful SS-9 proved it. CIA had been addressing this question repeatedly for several years and each time had reached the conclusion that they were not. Keep in mind that "first strike" in strategic terms does not simply mean, "strike a first blow." It means strike a first blow so devastating that your opponent cannot retaliate with greater force than you can withstand or absorb. CIA could find no evidence that the USSR could achieve such a position in the foreseeable future and did not believe that the SS-9 could provide it. The Air Force dissented as usual.

In the summer of 1969 a short study, titled "Memorandum to Holders," was prepared to update the most recent national estimate on Soviet weaponry. In a short paragraph that merely restated the conclusion of the detailed analysis in the estimate,

CIA reaffirmed its view that the USSR was not striving for a first-strike capability. Secretary Laird immediately took personal issue. He was about to make a speech in which he would proclaim that an ABM system was essential to combat the looming Soviet first strike. This was to be a U.S. policy statement, and he could not tolerate its denial by another U.S. government agency. Director Richard Helms received his request, consulted advisers, found that the CIA view was clearly stated in the current national estimate to which the present memorandum was a mere addendum, saw no need to flaunt the position simultaneously with the secretary's speech, and withdrew the short paragraph. Thomas Hughes, then head of State Department intelligence, put it back as a footnote regretting the omission.

The reaction among CIA analysts and estimators was intense. As they saw it, one of CIA's fundamental strengths had been violated: the right to state forthrightly any conclusion their intelligence led to regardless of existing U.S. policy. To them, Secretary Laird had confused the distinction between intelligence and policy, privileged governmental communication and public relations. Until this time, secretaries of state and defense, and presidents, too, had listened with equanimity to intelligence findings that ran cross-wise to U.S. policy and then proceeded as they saw fit. But to Secretary Laird, at this moment point man for the Nixon administration, a contrary view—even in a Top Secret paper—approached disloyalty. "Whose team is CIA on?" he was said to have asked.

My own reaction to Secretary Laird's unjustifiable action was not as explosive as the analysts' reaction. However much one would like to stand fast on principle on one front, there were dozens of other fronts remaining. If CIA was to retain its reputation for objectivity and credibility, it could not shoot the works and make a do-or-die stand on a single judgment even though the secretary of defense had egregiously misconstrued that finding as a policy statement. We could not afford to be seen by the administration as advocates for a controversial view. We were still in business and still had our job to do, serving the president to the best of our ability.

This personal resolution was severely shaken, however, by the Nixon administration's next move. Henry Kissinger declared that he and his NSC staff were going to examine the intelligence regarding the SS-9 themselves and arrive at their own conclusion. In other words, the CIA was no longer viewed as an independent voice, reporting directly to the president as his objective observer. We had been relegated to the outer ring of partisans, holding to views antithetical to the Nixon administration for some reason, historical (the "Missile Gap"?), personal, institutional, or whatever.

Dick Helms sent me along with Abbott Smith, head of the Office of National Estimates, to confer with Kissinger. We found him in an aggressive, nonconciliatory mood. He opened his copy of the paper and said something about its "bias." I objected to the term, and Kissinger responded, "Of course it's biased." He read a sentence describing the SS-9's performance. As I listened I heard through the rich, Germanic accent the tortured phrasing that reflected the intense struggle of the coordination meetings, the pulling and hauling between the Pentagon and CIA. Honesty forced me to admit that for someone reading it for the first time it could easily sound prejudiced, "biased." Abbott Smith offered to recast that portion and others that bothered Kissinger. We withdrew but learned in a few days that we had not shaken White House determination to examine the intelligence independently. There is some satisfaction in reporting that after a thorough review the NSC staff made no change in CIA's assessment of the SS-9's capabilities. It is also satisfying to record that the CIA view that the Soviets did not have a MIRV capability in 1969 and would not have one for five years was borne out in 1974 when the USSR tested its first MIRV.

Our next bruising encounter with the Nixon administration arose over Cambodia. We had known for several years that North Vietnamese army and Viet Cong units frequently slipped across the border into Cambodia for sanctuary while resting, resupplying, and refitting. We were also aware that supplies were coming down from North Vietnam into Cambodia. In a way almost exactly parallel to the controversy over enemy strengths, strong disagreement arose between MACV in Saigon and CIA in Washington over how much materiel was coming through the port of Sihanoukville. Just as in the previous conflict, neither side could claim conclusive evidence. CIA analysts, led by Paul Walsh, believed that enemy logistic requirements were being substantially met in shipments down the Ho Chi Minh Trail. Therefore, in analyzing the low-grade reports— again mostly prisoner-of-war interrogations, always unreliable— they established a minimal figure for Sihanoukville. The military in Saigon came up with a figure almost exactly double. There was some heat on CIA to resolve this difference because the Nixon administration had fastened on Cambodia as a major problem and was giving growing signs of wanting to do something about it. The command in Saigon held aggressively and tenaciously to its figure, which to us looked to be floating in midair, totally unsupported. Did they have information we did not have?

I went out to Saigon to find out and sat down with the military analysts to go over their data. The young officers were quiet-mannered and extremely modest about their supply figure. And with good reason: their evidence was exactly the same as ours, shoddy, low-grade reports. When I pressed hard as to how they supported their estimate, modesty began to approach embarrassment. They had nothing else to go on; the figure they produced was a possibility. I returned to Washington, and we reaffirmed the CIA view that military supplies moving through Sihanoukville were about half of MACV's estimate.

Then, a short time later, the roof fell in. The CIA clandestine service had succeeded in recruiting an agent with access to shipping and warehousing data. With meticulously recorded entries, the agent established without cavil that the correct figure was *much* higher than the one we held. Worse, it was almost the same as MACV's snatched-from-thin-air figure. I reported the new figure, with appropriate chagrin, to Dick Helms at the morning meeting. Cool as usual, he accepted it without flinching and directed us to do a post-mortem on the misjudgment. When it was completed he sent it on to the White House, which had, of course, been told at once of our discovery.

210

Our explanation was not satisfactory to President Nixon and Henry Kissinger. It was evident that they interpreted the mistake as further evidence of CIA bias, and it was murmured that we were advocates of the "McNamara position," whatever that was. The White House directed the President's Foreign Intelligence Advisory Board to conduct an inquiry. I presented our story to the team, which included a tall, striking blond woman, Nancy Maginnes, who later became Mrs. Henry Kissinger. Neither Miss Maginnes nor the other members of the PFIAB appeared to find our account convincing. Perhaps they expected us to apologize and confess. We did neither. We had made the best judgment we could with the evidence we had at the time. When better evidence came along, we immediately accepted it. No intelligence service can be asked to do more.

Perhaps the final blow to Nixon White House–CIA relations came over Chile. It is a story of which I know only the beginning because I had already made plans to leave Washington in the summer of 1971. Sometime in the autumn of 1970 I began to take stock of my role as DDI and the future of my CIA career. In early 1971 I would have been DDI for five years. Retirement was at least three years away, and although my predecessor, Robert Amory, had held the post for nine years, I had no wish to match him. In truth, I was beginning to flag. For one thing, I had made what changes in the directorate that had seemed desirable, and I was, in effect, just running the store. Perhaps a more compelling reason for thinking of change was one I was loath to admit even to myself, something I kept tucked in the back of my mind. I was weary of slogging against the suspicion and animus of the Nixon White House. It was in the air. When I did not experience it immediately I could see it in the strained face of Dick Helms as he recounted in the morning meeting his previous day's session with the president. Helms never openly complained or said anything to reveal the rough road he was traveling, but his face told the story to us who knew him.

It began to seem that we were starting all over again. We were no less competent than we had been in the glory days of the Cuban missile crisis or the Rolling Thunder analysis or the Arab-Israeli Six-Day War, but we were mistrusted. We were merely another of the many partisans who hungrily encircled the White House ramparts. Our judgments had no more value, indeed less, than that of the most junior analyst on Henry Kissinger's staff. Having established a respected place on the high ground of technical skill and objective, disinterested judgment during the Eisenhower, Kennedy, and Johnson administrations, we were now back at the bottom with all the hill to climb again. I had no appetite for the long climb.

I did not voice these innermost thoughts to anyone, but after thinking about it carefully I went to see Dick Helms one day. "I want you to understand," I said, "that I am not in any way complaining or asking to be relieved, but I just want to tell you that if you have any desire to replace me as DDI I would be agreeable. I have been in the job five years and will have been at least eight if I stay on to retirement. I don't think deputy directors ought to be lifetime appointments; you should be able to make changes whenever you wish. I have made all the innovations that I can think of. Maybe someone new will do better."

Helms thanked me for the offer and said he would like to think it over. Did I have any particular new assignment in mind? No, I replied, anything he wanted me to do. There were several places in headquarters where I could perhaps be useful, possibly the Office of National Estimates. But I rather thought I would like to go overseas again before I retired. "Let me think about it," Helms said.

Several months passed, and during that time the situation in Chile grew more disturbing, especially to the Nixon White House. CIA analysts had been warning for nearly a year that the success of Chilean leftists in exploiting the declining economic situation was causing the future of democratic government to look bleak. When the White House requested our judgment about the forthcoming autumn elections, we responded that the rightist candidate, Alessandri, and the leftist choice, Allende, appeared to be in a tight horse race that neither could win by a majority, thus throwing the result into the hands of the Congress where Allende's adherents might prevail. So likely did this outcome seem to our Latin American experts that we prepared another paper assessing the reaction throughout Latin America to an Allende assumption of power. As all the world later learned during the Watergate hearings, the possibility that Allende might take over Chile so alarmed President Nixon (who viewed Allende as a crypto-communist) that he ordered Helms and the CIA to undertake all possible covert action to prevent it.

In the upshot, Allende won by a narrow plurality that the Chilean congress confirmed. Allende held office for three years and was overthrown and slain by Chilean military officers. My personal knowledge of all this is scarcely greater than that of the average American. Whatever orders passed from President Nixon to Helms to the CIA covert action officers were transmitted in accordance with standard need-to-know principles. They were not known outside the Directorate of Operations except by inference. DDI analysts became aware through their day-to-day business with the operators that some sort of anti-Allende effort was under way, but to the analysts the leftist tide was running so strongly in Chile that such a belated undertaking looked feckless. When Allende did in fact ascend to the presidency I became aware that in White House eyes this was both another sign of CIA bias and a demonstration of incompetency. As an agency, CIA had predicted a leftist triumph, contrary to the expectations and hopes of the Nixonites, and then to compound the transgression CIA had only half-heartedly, or incompetently, tried to prevent what it had predicted would happen. Any understanding that CIA was not a monolith, that its analysts and operators might have opposing views, totally eluded the White House, just as it usually eluded the media and most outside observers. Whatever remaining confidence the White House retained in CIA was drained off by Chile.

My perception of this latest slump in CIA stock reinforced my feeling that the time had come to leave. Until the Nixon administration came to Washington, my work in CIA had always been fun, zesty, and fulfilling. Even in the early days, when we were building and acquiring skills, we had at worst experienced only inattention. But now, after a decade of demonstrated competence and dispassionate objectivity, we were suddenly seen as partisan and biased. The wholesome relationship between the White House and CIA had been replaced with sour distrust. It was an atmosphere that robbed the work of pleasure and satisfaction.

Several months after our first discussion Dick Helms called me in. "I've been thinking about your offer, which I genuinely appreciate," he said. "I've looked around here for what else you might do, and I find that you've already held the jobs I might want you to take." He went on to refer to my interest in going overseas and suggested I might take a senior job available in India as special assistant to the ambassador. I would have to transfer to the Department of State, but a three-year assignment would round out my government career. I asked for a few days to think it over and discuss it with my wife.

In the end I took the post in India, despite several middle-of-the-night spasms of uncertainty—"My God, what have I done!"—and Rosemary and I spent three always engrossing and often entrancing years in that fascinating and baffling country. The work was as different to me as the alien landscape and culture, but it became entirely rewarding and a wonderful end-piece to my career as a government servant.

It was in New Delhi, sitting in the U.S. Embassy, Edward Durrell Stone's practice run before designing the Kennedy Center in Washington, that I read in the pages of the *New York Herald Tribune*, Paris edition, of Richard Helms's dismissal from CIA. To me, it was the ultimate step in the trend I had watched beginning in 1968. To Ambassador Daniel Patrick Moynihan, a Nixon appointee and former White House staffer, it was puzzling. "Why was Helms fired?" he asked Henry Kissinger during a consultation visit in Washington.

"I didn't do it," replied Kissinger, "the *Chermans* did it." The drollery was delicious, and it is probable that Haldeman and Ehrlichman did take an active role in the action, but it is at best a partial truth. It was the mind-set of the Nixon White House that fired Richard Helms and precipitated the denigration of CIA. It was the mean-spirited, trust-no-one-but-ourselves, us-against-them siege mentality of Richard Nixon and his clique that did it.

In the months to come the pages of the *Herald Tribune* unfolded the sorry Watergate story, and I read with dismay the daily accounts of congressional hearings whose initial purpose was to establish CIA's official connection, or nonconnection, with the Watergate break-in but gradually transformed itself into an all-purpose exposure of CIA's derelictions over twenty-five years with one senator leading the hunt for the "rogue elephant" CIA had supposedly become and another peering suspiciously about for the "animals" he could "hear moving around in the forest." Nine thousand miles away, I was swept by conflicting feelings: anger over the prosecutory bias of the congressional inquisitors; frustration over my inability to combat the flood of half-truths and distortions of the media; and sympathy for my former colleagues, those who were trying to hold the Agency together in the midst of baleful confusion, and even more for my former chief, Dick Helms, who was constantly shuttling back and forth on the eighteen-hour flight from his post as ambassador in Tehran and required to recall the exact circumstances of an action taken five, ten, fifteen years before; and then, mingled wonder and relief that in some mysterious way I had decided at just the right moment to leave the post that would have placed me in the thick of the bloody fight.

But, even though valid, it was not a comfortable sense of relief. CIA had meant too much to me, my service had filled too large a space in my life and had given me too much fulfillment to permit me to be happy about being a mere spectator during the Agency's severest trial. In New Delhi, I could do nothing at the time, but it was then that I resolved someday to write a book that sought to provide a more accurate perspective. Perhaps in that way I could relieve in part my own sense of inadequacy in failing to be an active participant. Perhaps also I could enable other Americans to understand better the valid purposes and pro-

215

cedures of their national intelligence organization. I knew I could not confront the innumerable allegations of wrong-doing one by one, but perhaps I could place the full range of the Agency's activities in better perspective. And so, this book is my version of that perspective: an inside view of the CIA I knew, one I helped in a modest way to shape during the twenty-seven years I devoted to its service.

Afterthoughts

12

Americans find it difficult to think clearly about espionage and intelligence. For one thing, they experience a lascivious delight in the derring-do that they imagine invests every hour and every day of intelligence work. This makes it hard to be serious and realistic about the true nature of intelligence, a fact that was brought home to me by the reaction of several literary agents when I was looking for a publisher for my novel, *The Secret War*. The book has at its kernel a fictional retelling of an incident with an historical counterpart, and I strove throughout to make the actions of the CIA characters as realistic as possible. But it did not fit the mold of the genre or contain the stereotypes of spy fiction. One agent told me it "sounded too bureaucratic," another that it did not have enough "sense of danger." I rebutted that anyone driving down the New Jersey Turnpike alongside an eighteen-wheel truck experiences greater danger than the average CIA officer does in his entire career. The remark was very satisfying to me, but it was not convincing to those who knew what Americans expected a book about CIA to contain.

This fantasy about CIA and intelligence—a world of dark alley murder, laser-lighted sex, and coups by the dozen—leads readily to another source of difficulty in thinking clearly about it: moral revulsion. Having savored the fictional thrills of Robert Ludlum, it is easy upon reflection to find such goings-on as un-American when transferred to the real world. Americans still cling to the myth of innocence and forthright behavior as the only standard for their government even though their own personal and business lives often lack such innocence. The actions of business competition are justified by "that's good business;" on the athletic field by "anything to win;" the "morality" of illicit drugs and sex by "everyone does it." But for the government of the United States to subvert citizens of another country into spying against their nation, or to skew an election in a foreign country by subsidizing anticommunist candidates, or to provide arms covertly to groups opposing antidemocratic forces—all this is somehow un-American and hard to accept as proper.

Actions must be examined in context. One can most clearly find sanction for such covert actions in wartime. Traditionally, nations used to declare war upon one another as a signal of their intent to kill and destroy the other's military forces and so damage their war-making ability as to cause a surrender. Under the sanction of war, young men were justified in killing one another by fair means or foul. This was the ultimate sanction, and it rested on the proposition that the nation was in danger. From it flowed subsidiary sanctions, justification for sabotage, malicious propaganda, and assassination, all in the name of defeating the enemy and preserving one's own country. It also justified censorship and surveillance and arrest of one's own citizens.

What most people do not recognize is the current face of international conflict. In these less orderly, less formal times, nations no longer declare war. The United States has not been in a formal state of war in nearly half a century. But it cannot be denied that the United States is involved in a worldwide struggle with the Soviet Union and has been since the end of World War II. In the 1950s this struggle was termed the Cold War, and it was fought

218

by the USSR through political subversion and by covert supply of arms and training to forces rebelling against legitimate governments. To American leaders at the time, the most feasible way to oppose this Soviet activity was not to declare war but to meet the Soviet covert action with covert counteraction. The most readily available organization for this was CIA.

In the grey area of international struggle short of declared war, the sanctions are not clearly defined, and the American leadership and its instrumental agent, CIA, have had to make ad hoc decisions as to what covert actions are permissible and which are not. In the Cold War atmosphere, when Greece, Italy, and France were all threatened by political subversion and Eastern Europe had fallen into Soviet hands, the fear of communist subversion in this country was strong. Though marked by occasional hysteria, it had a genuine and valid base. In these circumstances the selective opening of mail from U.S. citizens to the USSR, or its return, was deemed justified by American leaders. The purpose was to identify Soviet subversive agents in the USSR and their tools in the United States. During World War II such activity would have seemed routine. In the Cold War it seemed justified. As it happened, the program remained active, though always on a small scale, beyond a time when there was general support for such activity. There had been a fundamental shift in American perception of the Soviet threat, its seriousness, and how to deal with it. In the great moral purgation attending the Watergate hearings the mail-opening program was exposed, and public outcry against this invasion of American citizens' rights was loud. CIA, the instrumental agent, was charged with the crime. The American leaders who had approved the program in the 1950s and the historical shift in the public's view of the Soviet threat both came off scot-free. Just as in other instances, this combination of the absence of formal sanction and shift in perspective regarding the threat left the Agency exposed.

Recent years have seen a running debate within American society over the need for covert action. Much of the discussion has seemed to me misguided, resting as it does either in some occasions on moral revulsion or on greater faith in its efficacy than history can justify. I would suggest that American experience with covert action since World War II has established that it can be useful to American interests only under the following conditions: (1) American policy regarding the issue must be unanimously approved within government and supported by a clear majority of the American people; (2) the main tools of this policy must be diplomatic or overtly military with covert action playing only a subordinate, supporting role; (3) the covert action contemplated must be kept small and feasibly deniable because otherwise it becomes self-defeating and inflicts great damage on the instrumental agent, CIA.

Violations of these principles have abounded in recent years. There has been no clear national consensus regarding U.S. policy in Latin America. Covert action has been required to take the major role, not the supporting one. The activities have been too visible for denial and have indeed damaged CIA. It must be admitted that it is hard to imagine that *any* covert action, large, small, or medium, could long remain deniable in the present poisonous atmosphere of Congress where it is subject to the scrutiny of the current oversight committees and their legions of staff. Apparently forgotten is the fact that a nation undertakes covert action when it wishes to avoid the risks of acting openly and possibly challenging directly a foreign power or wishes to prevent the group it is supporting from being identified as a tool of American policy. Without these three requirements, covert action is unnecessary or unwise; when they are lacking or removed by irresponsible public debate, the nation looks extraordinarily foolish.

In the years since World War II, the United States has come to terms with the unremitting threat of the Soviet Union. Though the menace is potentially greater now than at any previous time, given the massive military power of the USSR as well as its ability to foster terrorism worldwide, we have learned to live with it day by day. But time has not lessened the need for vigilance. Nor has it diminished the broader requirements for understanding both the

220

promise and the danger flowing from the ferment and the turbulence of the rest of the world. We are experiencing a far-reaching, historic transition in worldwide power relationships, a transition that must inevitably touch the United States in a multitude of ways. Together, the threat and the promise validate the need, perhaps more strongly than ever, for a competent national intelligence system. Properly led, appropriately supported, and sensibly monitored, CIA can provide the external vigilance essential to the nation's security.